pppeeeaaaccceee

Coach House Books

copyright © Darren O'Donnell, 2003

first edition

Published with the assistance of the Canada Council for the Arts and the Ontario Arts Council

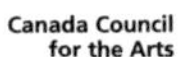

We also acknowledge the Government of Ontario through the Ontario Book Publishers Tax Credit program and through the Ontario Book Initiative.

NATIONAL LIBRARY OF CANADA CATALOGUING IN PUBLICATION

O'Donnell, Darren, 1965-
Pppeeeaaaccceee / Darren O'Donnell.

A play.

ISBN 1-55245-121-6

I. Title. II. Title: Peace.

PS8579.D64P64 2003 C812'.6 C2003-901439-8
PR9199.4.036P64 2003

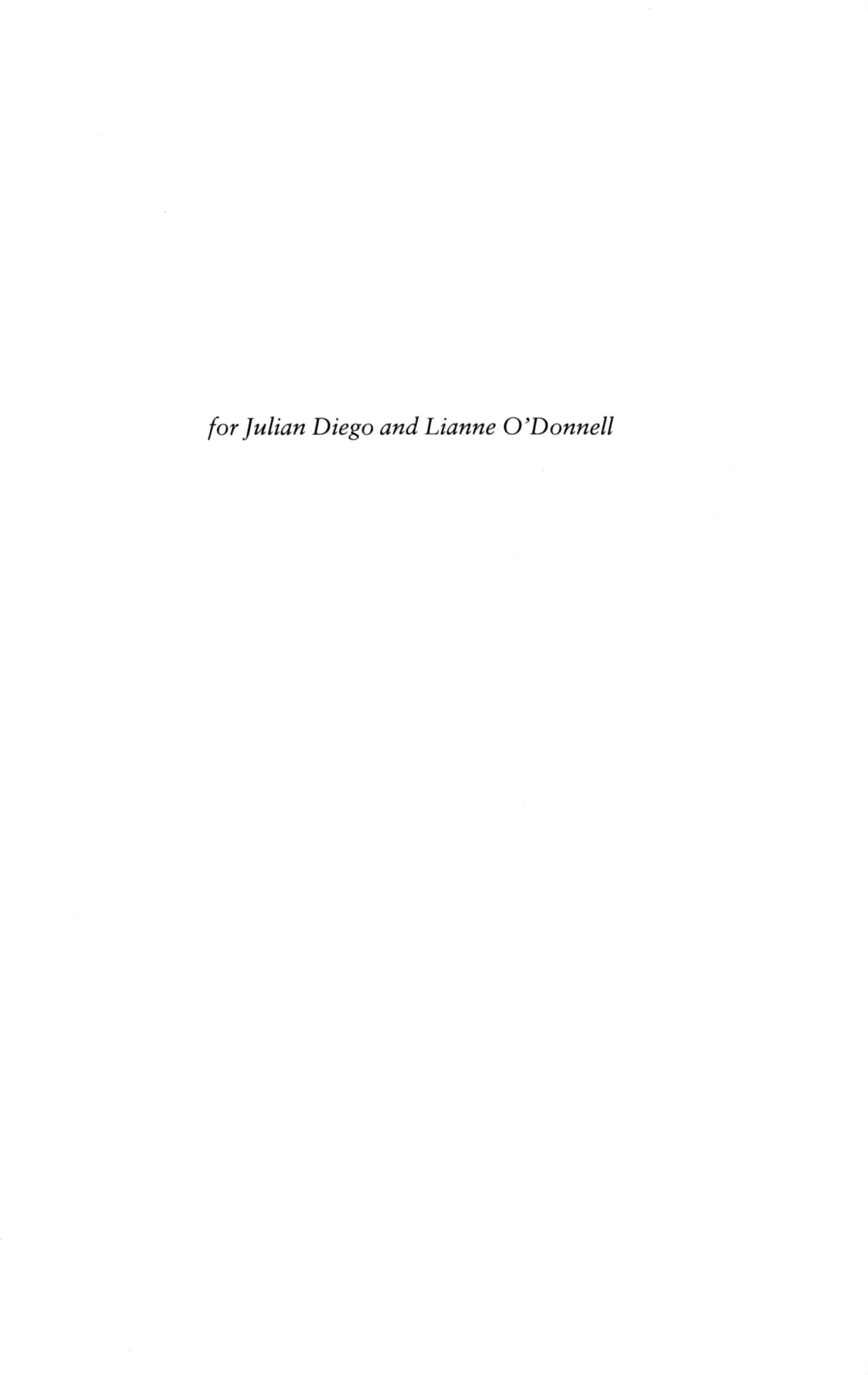

for Julian Diego and Lianne O'Donnell

Contents

A Foreword

by Daniel MacIvor

Sandwich.

Just 'sandwich.'

pppeeeaaaccceee is a sandwich.

Two pieces of bread, some mustard, a little mayonnaise, a tomato slice and the meat (or Textured Vegetable Protein for those of that persuasion).

The first piece of bread is the room.
It could be a theatre – either large or small –
or it could be a living room or a kitchen.
If it's a theatre it has to be welcoming and warm, with beautiful light –
the light of the sun and the moon mixed with a candle and a touch of streetlamp light through a window –
and there must be some kind of backdrop,
preferably looking like it was made from clouds, but sturdy enough to climb,
as one might climb into a dream or a lover.
If the room is a kitchen there should be some dishes in the sink,
and if the room is a living room there should be cushions on the floor,
and there shouldn't be a television anywhere nearby,
even off,
even turned toward the wall.
In the kitchen or the living room the talking should either:
start while it's still light outside and end when the moon is up,
or,
begin in the candlelit darkness and complete when morning fills the corners.

The second piece of bread is the people talking.
These can be any three people at all,
as long as they are the three most special people on earth.
These three people should know how contentment smells, where
sorrow comes from, why laughter is sad, and be very, very
suspicious of applause.
They should love cats and/or dogs and/or
shed even just one salty tear whenever they eat a fish.
They should know that anger never owns us, it just visits.
And they should always, always, no matter who, no matter what,
no matter when or what height, always look it in the eye.
They should also understand that irony is sharp and doesn't taste
very good, and that it's surprise that keeps us alive.
Finally, and firstly, the idea is not lost on them that 'together'
breaks down into 'to' and 'get' and 'her' and if there is a God (like
the God people talk about beyond all the regular gods) she's
probably a woman, and
getting
her
is all about getting
together.

The mustard is the magic.
The mayonnaise is the coincidence.

(And of course once the magic and the coincidence are mixed
together it's very hard to tell where the mustard ends and the
mayonnaise begins.)

The meat (or TVP if such is your predilection) is the people
watching and listening. Now if we're in a theatre, this is where
things can get confusing, because some will watch and some will
listen and many will neither and few will both –
and there's not much one can do about that other than to put a
warning on the ticket or require entrance exams to the festivities.

But if at all possible it would be best to assemble a public not
foreign to the following:
laugher, awe, head nodding, bemused brow furrowing, bliss,
gladness, joy, despair and mistiness
(as in mistablility – as in an openness to throat-lumping and
happy-tearing).
At least of all leasts it is essential that these people are the kind of
people who do not hold their breath when they
close their eyes
and they must not be afraid to smile.
Now if we're in a kitchen or a living room, it is not necessary that
there be any people watching or listening other than the people
talking –
which I think is a phenomenon once called
'conversation.'
This can be very nice, this can be beautiful and true and might
change something forever,
something small but something forever.

Oh, and the tomato slice is a gift for the gods, because tomato is a
nightshade and as we all know the gods love their nightshades.
(I mean the regular gods not the God god people talk about,
because who really knows what she really loves other than
herself and us.)

Gosh, I better go now.
All this talk about sandwiches is making me hungry.

Abiquiu, New Mexico
February 14, 2003

About the Play

by Darren O'Donnell

I'm writing this introduction ten days after *pppeeeaaaccceee* was presented over four days in the 2003 Six Stages Festival in Toronto. Working on a show for more than three years, teching it for two days, then performing it for four is like taking three years to prepare to be shot out of a cannon: really nice except for those last few seconds, about which I can remember next to nothing. If I recall correctly, there was the sound of wind whistling in my ears.

A half-hour version of *pppeeeaaaccceee* was written in 1999 for the 2000 Rhubarb! Festival in response to a conversation I had in the summer with my friend Julian Diego on the patio of the Last Temptation in Kensington Market. I wanted to replicate the listening, respect and speculation that were particularly strong that afternoon. In keeping with the conversation, I also wanted to create a play that didn't need to resort to character, plot or conflict. This urge comes from a frustration and fatigue I feel with much of the theatre that is being produced around these parts. A lot of my friends who work in other media often tell me they don't attend theatre not only because is it usually bad but also because they often find themselves embarrassed for those onstage. When pressed, they tend to

articulate a discomfort at theatre's unwillingness to let go of an artifice, a pretending and an insistence on trying to represent 'real' people experiencing 'real' conflict – a kind of representation that most other mediums have carefully dismantled, if not entirely left behind. Not that theatre hasn't explored other avenues, but too often the individual and her struggles are still very central, when, to my mind, there are bigger, more urgent things to question – an important one being the very existence of the idea of the individual itself; how to recognize that we're always much more and much less than we imagine we are. With *pppeeeaaaccceee*, I wanted to situate the conflict between the audience and the material, feeling that was a more honest approach.

This desire to shake up standard ideas of what I suppose can be reduced to self and other led me to disrupt my habit of working with the kind of sparring polarities that had dominated *White Mice, Boxhead, Over* and *Who Shot Jacques Lacan?*. I decided to create a piece for three voices and I started by simply writing without assigning identities of any sort to the characters – no names, no race, no gender, nothing. I knew I was writing for at least two women of colour, and I didn't want to anticipate which lines any of them would speak, hoping to create something that would transcend my own limited perspectives. In 2001, on the day before one of the workshops, I stayed up until all night going through the script and assigning lines to each of the actors, hoping that, with a particular actor in mind, the words would be filed according to my intuitive response to what I knew of the actors' personalities. I think it worked out well – that the individuation of the characters is accomplished by the force of the actors' personalities. It was to this end that I maintained the actors' names in the script and, while directing, insisted the actors were simply playing themselves saying the lines.

The dialogue itself also represents an attempt to circumvent my tendency to tell a certain kind of story that I'm starting to dislike: people opposing each other, all driving toward some representation of catharsis or transformation which never actually occurs anywhere.

One key to understanding the movement of the dialogue, then, is that I was trying to illustrate the mind's tendency toward associative thinking – arguably a weak way to go through life but a popular one nonetheless. Often, topic shifts hinge on the characters' interest in talking about their own experiences, prompted, sometimes, by simply a word from the others: 'You look classy when you pun,' 'I didn't know I was working class until someone handed me a shovel.' This, it seems to me, is more accurate than any single-tack, coherent conversation in a conventional play, and it presented a challenge to me; to keep the audience interested as the dialogue drifts across subjects, through the course of a night, seemed to demand some kind of through line, or at least a trajectory. This led to organizing the material based on the structure of the dark night of the soul – a cyclical movement which I assume most people experience (I can experience a few rounds even within the course of a single day). In *pppeeeaaaccceee*, it sees the characters lose faith in the world, themselves, and then, finally, in the possibility of true contact with each other, followed immediately by the sunrise. It's an emotional trajectory, not an intellectual one, and to try to understand it rationally should, I hope, be frustrating. The various incidents that serve as skeletal plot points – 'pipsqueaks,' 'creatures,' and the sleeping sequences – all serve allegorical functions and their meaning should be multivalent, though it is important to note that the characters live in a world where the division between dreaming and awake and dead and alive has been breached. The creatures are most definitely in the characters' heads. The problem is, the characters' heads are everywhere.

I'm always trying to transform the audience's consciousness, sometimes through information, as with *White Mice,* and sometimes, as with *pppeeeaaaccceee*, through the actual encounter with the play. The first half of the show is intended to overwhelm the viewer's rational mind by providing a complicated labyrinth of information, anecdotes, observations and activities. I hoped that willing audience members would happily give up on any attempts to follow the story, sort the information or rationalize the experience in any way. Like my process in writing the play, I trusted that the play's cohesion rested on its appeal to an intuitive understanding of the proceedings, in the same way that meditation, work with a mantra, or physical

L to R: Greg MacArthur, Ngozi Paul,
Maiko Bae Yamamoto, Darren O'Donnell (floor)

work such as tai chi will short-circuit the obsessively rational head brain, leaving the body – a much wiser instrument and, arguably, a brain in itself – to do the thinking. In the second half of the play, beginning with the clove cigarette, I inject the two main thematic points: the first contained in Ngozi's sandwich and the subsequent fortune cookie, and the second in the story of the non-existent lover and Maiko's dream.

Invoking an amorphous and ill-defined revolution serves a variety of purposes, some contradictory. The world is a terrible place of limited options, incredible excesses and deficiencies, of inequities and an ever-increasingly rampant soullessness – or at least that's how it looks to me. I don't attribute this to any natural tendency on the part of humanity toward greed; I believe most people are generous and willing to share but, simply, there are a few – a very few – who want it all and will go to any lengths to get it. Now more than ever, there's a critical mass of people living in both economic and spiritual poverty, but the idea of sudden social change becomes ever more difficult to imagine. The revolution of the play tries to tease the audience, inviting the question 'What revolution?' A good question.

My own hope is for revolution in the way people relate to each other – a sudden spreading wildfire of respectful listening and kindness which would grip the populace with the possibility of loving contact. And from there, who knows how far we could go? A naïve and immature desire, I guess, but it's something I can't help but deeply yearn for.

pppeeeaaaccceee, through its attempt to include the active participation of the audience's imagination, proposes a kind of entertainment that, while remaining something at which to passively stare, tries to engage the onlooker's mind, body and soul. I want people to leave the theatre and talk to each other in new ways, in ways that enjoy ambiguity and confusion, that don't look to understand but are happy to just be. I want to circumvent the tendency to evaluate the show as good or bad and offer as revolutionary the possibility that some things are both at the same time. Sometimes I watched the show and felt the characters were beautifully utopian in their kindness toward each other – something I was sometimes intending – but other times I felt they were totally in denial, obliviously self-deceiving creatures living an obvious fiction: liars. Responses from my friends ranged widely – some seeing the play as a demonstration in respect and some finding a subversive satirical intent in the play. I wanted both. That the cast looked like a Benetton ad is no accident.

Ultimately, the show is a series of naive questions, observations and experiments – a naïveté easily dismissed by the cynical. I'm looking for a new kind of subversion which enters through the back door, not by angrily or tiredly pointing to all the horrors power has created in the world – everybody already knows about all that shit – but, instead, with a sense of high naïveté which attacks a hip irony with sincerity, hoping the ironic is consumed by an impossible sense of earnestness, yielding the sensation that hope may be found by accepting – if only for a moment – the hopelessness of the situation. Hiding in the fortune cookie is the assertion that for love to make any difference in this idiotic world, it's going to have to make do with nothing, with no one, not even yourself. Then, maybe we can kick some ass.

The response to the show has been strongly divided. When trying to account for this, Yvonne Ng, the artist responsible for the show's graphic featured on the book's cover, observed that because the show is so flat – so 2D, with no plot or conflict and barely the trace of character, much like the innocence of her felt drawing – it functions as a mirror in which the audience will tend to see the state of their own spirit, some finding it to be an aggressive and pretentious display and some seeing a generous humility. Again, I'm hoping for both.

A good friend took big exception to what he called the Post-Modern Stuff: a deconstructed beginning, a lecture on performance, the silent beat, a lecture on applause and the 'idiot' section, which he took to be a taunt of the audience. He asked, 'Why lecture me about the nature of performance the way you did at the top of the show unless you think I've never been to the theatre before? ... I know it's fake. Theatre is fake.' In response, I stated that pointing out that the words were not written by the actors was not intended to be a big revelation – it was simply a fact. But we seem to be living in a social climate where pointing out the small obvious things – the sky is blue, the rich are getting richer and the poor are getting poorer – can be interpreted as an act of aggression. I know you know the actors didn't write the words, and to acknowledge it is not some act of arch-cleverness but an attempt at a naked naïveté that tries to let out all the air of the pretentiousness – or pretendingness – of the theatrical experience while still being unable or unwilling to give up the game. Some people will find this, in itself, pretentious. All of the Post-Modern Stuff in the show is only charming in its transparency and its familiarity. It's not new, it's not fancy, it – like the show's graphic – is warm, fuzzy and sweet as hell, but, admittedly, if you look carefully, you'll notice the children's eyes are red and the representation of Maiko is suffering from decapitation; it's a fine line where I hope to unearth some fertile contradictions. As I said to my friend, if the Post-Modern Stuff in the show incites huffiness, crossed arms and a declaration that it's not going to fool anyone, then the trap has been sprung and, by the gods and in the most loving way, I believe we've caught ourselves a pipsqueak.

While a sincere attempt at naïveté as subversive strategy could be considered a foolish risk, I believe a bigger risk is in trying to create something intended to defy description. Not so good for the box office. In this world, if you can't sum it up in a sentence, people don't want to hear about it. I want people to try to describe the show to their friends only to stop in frustration and insist that the only way to deal with it is to experience it themselves. That also leaves the work vulnerable, and the critical response, too, has been fiercely divided – something I consider, in theory anyway, to be the hallmark of success, as hard as it is to deal with in practice. Defying description serves both an aesthetic and a political purpose; in a world rapidly backing away from notions of contradiction, paradox and ambiguity in favour of embracing simplistic, false and dangerous dichotomies such as Right vs. Wrong, Good vs. Evil and Heaven vs. Hell, I feel creating work that defies description offers support for views that are, ultimately, generous and inclusive.

However, there's a specificity in the play which, I believe, grounds it in a particular place and time and which seeks a specific audience. This kind of ambiguity and love of contradiction and confusion is not for everyone and not for every situation. Like all my writing, it functions as a call to others, not so much to rally together under a particular banner, but in the case of *pppeeeaaaccceee*, to identify who is interested, able and willing to stand with me and embrace a love of confusion, excluding those who aren't, can't or won't.

Why all this explaining? Why not let the play speak for itself? I wanted to provide a context for the work because, unfortunately, I don't believe anyone else is doing it. In the last two decades, the social significance of theatre has waned drastically, overtaken by the exploding proliferation of interest in and opportunities for film and video. And because theatre deftly and, perhaps sadly, avoids commodification – you can't record it and mass-produce it in any way – it has ceased to be something that people who want to talk to the world are interested in. So, the discourse about theatre, around these parts, anyway, has shrivelled to almost nothing; practitioners and critics alike have very little context with which to look at the work and very little idea what is happening elsewhere or in other related media, and nobody is talking about theatre like it matters. Personally, I don't know if it really matters. I just like the power of being in the same room with people, accomplishing something together in real time and talking about it afterwards. This introduction is intended to initiate a discussion of the work and to invite those who work in theatre to talk about why we continue to care when so few others do.

I hope *pppeeeaaaccceee* is not finished. With only five performances over four days, there are a lot of people who didn't get a chance to see it, and I hope to revisit the script, responding to the comments and criticisms of friends and colleagues. This book was conceived to be a document of the time we had mounting this version; if you feel like commenting on this draft or checking out possible subsequent drafts, please drop me a line at darren@mammalian.ca.

Finally, if you're interested in producing *pppeeeaaaccceee* or using it in a scene study class or whatever, I would ask you to respect the original impulse and cast no more than one man and one white person. Beyond that, how you cast is your business: Maiko can be a black man, Ngozi a white woman and Greg a First Nations woman, or they can all be black women – it doesn't matter as long as you respect the formula: no more than one man, no more than one whitey. If this is a challenge, then all the more reason to give it a try.

Thanks.

L to R: Greg MacArthur, Maiko Bae Yamamoto, Ngozi Paul, Darren O'Donnell

pppeeeaaaccceee

A Performance History

pppeeeaaaccceee was co-produced by Mammalian Diving Reflex and the Six Stages Festival and premiered by the Festival at Theatre Passe Muraille in January 2003.

Greg: Greg MacArthur
Ngozi: Ngozi Paul
Maiko: Maiko Bae Yamamoto

Written and directed by Darren O'Donnell
Produced by Naomi Campbell

Lighting design: Rebecca Picherack
Sound design and operation: murr
Set design: Darren O'Donnell and Naomi Campbell
Choreography: Sarah Chase
Costume design: Nina Okens
Assistant directors: Troy O'Donnell and Nicole Stamp
Stage management and light operation: John Patrick Robichaud
Technical direction: Trevor Schwellnus

A collaboration between Darren O'Donnell and producer Naomi Campbell, Mammalian Diving Reflex is firmly constituted to alter audience consciousness, creating theatre that is at once furious, riotous and rigorous. Mammalian Diving Reflex smashes ideas together at high speeds to see what pops out, inadvertently producing ideal entertainment for the end of the world.

Set

A huge piece of spandex on which the actors stand that stretches from the front of the stage back and up to the grid. Midstage is an 8´ x 4´ riser hidden beneath the spandex which the actors sit on. Behind the riser and still under the spandex is a 12´ ladder which the actors climb on.

Light

Constantly shifting, lots of saturated colours, some swirling gobos, warm atmosphere for the most part. The action of the play travels through the course of a night, so the light should reflect that journey while not being tied to it.

Sound

Mellow late-night radio, an electronic score that supports the action and some real sounds: crickets and cityscape. These intertwine and wind through the show.

Costumes

Nothing special. Ordinary hanging-out-with-your-friends kind of clothing. Bare feet. There may be some kind of material incorporated into the clothing that occasionally emits light, so that the body within appears to be glowing through the seams.

Choreography

Simple gestures that repeat and, depending on the context, can take on a variety of meanings, ultimately suggesting that the three characters' individuality is shared.

Acting

Simple, innocent and generous. Some sections are clearly and deliberately narration while others are clearly conversation; the distinction is fluid and seamless. There is a constant oscillation between speaking to the audience – sometimes even quietly acknowledging laughter with the occasional smile – and speaking to each other. They are often very open about the fact that they're just up there talking, and then they are sometimes completely engulfed in the world, oblivious to the audience.

pppeeeaaaccceee

As the audience enters, the actors slowly drift from backstage to eventually stand downstage centre. As they walk, they talk amongst themselves, occasionally glancing at the audience with gentle curiosity. If they see a friend and they feel like waving or saying hi, they do. They remain casual. There is the sound of a machine in the distance and the spandex is illuminated with colours that slowly shift. The show is already underway. When the house closes, JP *signals the actors to begin. The sound changes, and the sound of crickets slowly creeps in.*

NGOZI: *(to* JP*)* Okay?

GREG: Hi.

MAIKO: Things are going to start in a sec.

GREG: Now might be a good time to turn off your cell phones or whatever else you have in your pockets.

NGOZI: *(to* JP*)* Are we okay?

JP: Standing by.

GREG: *(to* JP*)* Thanks.

NGOZI: Okay.

MAIKO: Hi. Okay, so, the desire here is to tell the truth about our situation in such a way as to keep you interested and, at the same time, touch you in ways that can't be entirely controlled, predicted, described, or, for that matter, understood.

GREG: So, that's the basic deal here.

NGOZI: Of course, to speak truthfully can be difficult – some say impossible – but possible or not, we're going to give it a shot.

(The house lights very slowly fade.)

MAIKO: The first truth wanting to be aired – and an obvious one at that – is that these words coming out of this mouth are not spontaneously occurring to this person here and now. This mouth simply delivers them to you.

NGOZI: There's the hope that on the way to you these words will be electrified by this mouth, this being, and by striking your being will yield unexpected sensations created by all of us at once together.

GREG : What's being sought is the blurring of common sense distinctions as we fade into each other during something that could be called the 'twilight of our being.'

NGOZI: That may sound frightening to you but in the long run it won't be.

MAIKO: Perhaps an imaginary group hug may be the best way to proceed.

GREG: Feel free to shut your eyes for a moment – go ahead. If you like. We'll make sure no one hits you.

NGOZI: Now. Imagine the entire room is hugging you, from all the other people to the bricks in the walls, down to the chair that is sucking gently on your bum. It's all hugging you.

MAIKO: Imagine for a moment that when the hug is at its most intimate you lose that sense of distinctness you hold close to what you call your own heart and everything bleeds into everything else.

GREG: While the sensation may be strange, there's nothing to fear. You won't disappear, you will not become nothing or no one.

MAIKO: Think of those times when you're in a room talking with a few friends as the sun goes down.

NGOZI: When it becomes dark before you realize it's dark.

GREG: As the light disappears, the faces of your friends appear to become the faces of strangers, right, or worse, they appear grotesque, monstrous.

MAIKO: You may experience a bit of terror.

NGOZI: A terror in response not only to the shifting faces of your friends but also to the alarming fact that you hadn't noticed the sun had gone down.

MAIKO: 'How could I have not noticed?' you might ask yourself. 'I've been left behind thinking it was day when all around me night has infiltrated.'

GREG: The first clue had been the strange faces that had taken over your friends, the kind of blurring that always happens when things are said to be in their twilight.

MAIKO: Do you think what you're experiencing is real?

NGOZI: Twilight is when the truth is always revealed.

MAIKO: It's twilight.

GREG: It is twilight.

MAIKO: It's a nice night.

NGOZI: It's a beautiful night.

GREG: It's a quiet night.

MAIKO: Let's see if we can find some true universal love songs.

NGOZI: All right.

(The actors perform a small piece of choreography. The music, Eddie Harris's 'The Things You Do,' starts.)

GREG: That's nice.

NGOZI: That is nice.

MAIKO: I feel like talking.

NGOZI: I feel like talking, too. Do you?

GREG: I do. What should we talk about?

MAIKO: I wouldn't mind talking about the revolution.

NGOZI: Do you want to talk about the revolution?

GREG: I guess for a while and then I'd like to stop.

NGOZI: Suddenly?

MAIKO: Suddenly we'll just stop talking when we've all had enough.

NGOZI: Okay.

GREG: What if we have enough at different times?

MAIKO: Well, the feeling of having enough will probably travel in cycles, right.

GREG: Okay.

MAIKO: We just have wait out any downturns until our cycles match and then we can stop.

GREG: Okay.

NGOZI: Okay.

MAIKO: Before the revolution the world had become a place I was unable to accurately describe.

GREG: But during the revolution the fundamentals became so crystal clear. For the first time in my life, anyway …

NGOZI: And since the revolution, there's a vagueness and a trust in something that shouldn't be reduced – can't be reduced – to words.

MAIKO: Before the revolution a few things had gone off the rails.

GREG: Absolutely obvious things like food, shelter and meaningful activities with which you could pass the day that didn't seem to involve doing things you would rather not.

NGOZI: I always felt like I was an integral part of some useless machine that used my body as a battery.

GREG: During the revolution I just remember how all my cells felt aligned toward a simple common purpose; fundamental contradictions were eradicated.

MAIKO: Before the revolution people treated each other with such contempt most of the time.

GREG: During the revolution you either treated people with a respect bordering on mania or you simply cut off their heads.

MAIKO: Before the revolution there was a glazed look on everybody's face – an angry look or a sad look, a hollow look.

GREG: Before the revolution everybody was always attempting to fuse into a scene, to become popular.

NGOZI: Popularity and relevance to the people were always getting confused.

MAIKO: Since the revolution there has been a machine created that flies around looking for people who aren't happy, snatches them up and creates pure happiness which it sprinkles onto the heads of the populace.

GREG: It's supposed to feel really good.

MAIKO: Loneliness is still okay, though. It's just a certain kind of redundant unhappiness that is discouraged.

GREG: Loneliness is a sign of intelligence.

NGOZI: Before the revolution they tried to round up all the intelligent people.

GREG: Before the revolution I once felt a Supreme Intelligence enter my life, a presence as large as seventy-two sneezes in a row.

MAIKO: That's big.

GREG: You're telling me – I had to wear a diaper.

NGOZI: Before the revolution I was once stalked by a Supreme Intelligence; it was always hanging out in my periphery.

MAIKO: I had a job once with a Supreme Intelligence.

GREG: How did it pay?

MAIKO: I was reimbursed in thought.

NGOZI: How was that?

MAIKO: Mind-boggling.

GREG: A boggled mind can be an asset.

MAIKO: You find?

GREG: Well, you're not as susceptible to the manipulations of advertisers.

MAIKO: That's true.

(The music and crickets fade.)

NGOZI: Though it is hard to have meaningful relationships with anybody other than the void.

MAIKO: And the void's never been very good in bed.

NGOZI: The void's not bad in bed.

MAIKO: No, it's not bad. It's just –

GREG: People are so much more exciting to have sex with.

MAIKO: Of course.

NGOZI: *(laughs affectionately)* People.

(Pause.)

MAIKO: I love people.

GREG: People are people.

NGOZI: Among other things.

MAIKO: Yes.

GREG: Before the revolution I had a hundred lovers. It was a festival of flesh.

NGOZI: Before the revolution I had a lover I couldn't shake. My lover was like a wart on my heart.

MAIKO: Before the revolution I had elevated being single to a science.

GREG: What were the tenets of your system?

MAIKO: Well, I found that singlehood could be maintained by rigorously keeping my politics shifting around the spectrum. I mapped all possible political positions according to all four points of the compass, plus the additional up and down, and then –

NGOZI: Could you show us in the air with your hand?

MAIKO: Sure. *(demonstrates)* All four points of the compass plus the additional up and down.

NGOZI: Right.

MAIKO: And then with my shifting beliefs I would try to create geometric shapes that would be interesting to myself only.

GREG: So?

MAIKO: So like this. *(demonstrates)* That way I never remained in one spot for any length of time so no one was able to relate to me for any length of time. As I and a potential lover would come in close to kiss, as I would feel the dew of their nose breath condensing on my upper lip, I would suddenly switch my entire belief system and they would find me untenable.

NGOZI: Were there not some people whose grasp of their own politics was so tentative that they would be willing to forgive even the most intolerable points of view?

MAIKO: Yes, I realized quickly that I would have to avoid the lightly convicted person, so I only dated fanatics.

GREG: Did you have to believe in things you didn't believe in?

MAIKO: Well, since a belief system is a shifting mix of ideas gleaned from contrasting the information from all your experiences with the information from all your experiences I just made sure I experienced nothing. I spent my entire time in a sensory deprivation tank.

NGOZI: It must have been hard to meet people.

MAIKO: Exactly.

GREG: And since the revolution?

MAIKO: Well, since the fundamental points of view have happily collapsed into one or two or whatever, people are trying to get into my pants all the time.

GREG: Nice.

MAIKO: I just go with the flow.

(Eddie Harris's 'The Things You Do' and crickets are re-established.)

NGOZI: I had a lover during the revolution.

GREG: I didn't know that.

NGOZI: Yeah.

GREG: Yeah?

NGOZI: It got really bad.

MAIKO: How?

NGOZI: It was – it was just terrible.

GREG: Do you still see them?

NGOZI: No.

GREG: Are they still alive?

(Pause.)

NGOZI: No.

MAIKO: Did you have to kill them?

(Long pause.)

NGOZI: No. Maybe. I don't know.

MAIKO: I'm sorry.

NGOZI: All I did was bolt the door. I was very frightened.

GREG: No surprise.

NGOZI: I guess not. I was always either over- or underestimating my own cowardice.

GREG: It was a hard thing to call.

MAIKO: I was a huge coward.

NGOZI: I was a superficial monster: all my actions came from the surface of the surface of the surface's surface.

GREG: Since we couldn't change the important things, it was the superficial things that occupied so much of our energy.

MAIKO: I lost a friend over the question of how to hold a spoon.

NGOZI: Exactly. You remember the famous revolutionary maxim 'the personal is political'?

GREG: Who can forget it.

NGOZI: Well, it seemed to take on a life of its own.

MAIKO: Yes.

NGOZI: How you brushed your teeth became an indicator of your political position.

MAIKO: Do you consider the revolution to have been a success?

NGOZI: Success?

MAIKO: Are you content with the way things are?

GREG: I believe so.

MAIKO: You?

NGOZI: Well, you know, contentment – no one ever promised me contentment.

MAIKO: No, that's true. I don't remember seeing contentment on my list of ingredients.

GREG: No, personally, I'm mostly composed of water.

MAIKO: Sometimes a gurgling brook sounds content.

NGOZI: The only time I've ever gurgled was when I tried to hang myself.

GREG: How did you botch it up?

NGOZI: Well, that was the thing that came between me and that lover. My lover denied me my right to end my life, something I fully consider 101. My lover cut me down and I cut my lover off.

MAIKO: Sent them packing?

NGOZI: Into the night.

GREG: What happened to them?

NGOZI: They were hanged.

MAIKO: I'm sorry, that's terrible.

NGOZI: It is. I miss them. I sometimes like to think that I can feel them in the room, that I can talk to them.

GREG: Do you feel like they're in the room right now?

NGOZI: No, I never feel like they're in the room; I just sometimes like to think I can feel them in the room.

MAIKO: The city's a big place. They could be in almost any room.

GREG: It is big.

NGOZI: I'm sure I'll encounter them again someday, somehow or other, even if it's just in the smallest of gestures that I accidentally acquired from them.

MAIKO: The way you wipe your nose?

NGOZI: Could be.

MAIKO: Brush your teeth?

NGOZI: They looked so funny when they brushed their teeth.

MAIKO: The way they said 'hi' to strangers.

NGOZI: I guess I could meet them almost anywhere.

(Music and crickets fade.)

GREG: Do you remember the way the revolution started?

NGOZI: I remember there was a lot of smoke.

MAIKO: There were burning buildings.

NGOZI: Things were collapsing.

MAIKO: The poor people had had enough.

GREG: Yeah, but we had had enough for a long time.

MAIKO: Maybe, but there were just more of us.

GREG: Yeah, that's true, but I'm talking about when the awareness of our poverty gained that new scope.

MAIKO: There was the thing with conversation.

GREG: Yeah, that was a significant shift.

NGOZI: It happened overnight.

MAIKO: We all knew that things had gone terribly, terribly wrong, that we were lied to, manipulated and ripped off at almost every turn.

GREG: That was almost universally understood.

NGOZI: The whole thing was murdering people left, right and centre but no one could agree on an enemy. Then overnight it changed, it became so apparent to so many people.

MAIKO: What did it was a serious and sudden decline in the art of conversation.

NGOZI: As the ranks of the elite became tighter and fewer, the more they pumped resources into keeping us distracted, so the quality of conversation dropped like a rock.

GREG: It was stunning.

MAIKO: Even the most shallow person became profoundly uneasy.

GREG: But at first no one was able to put their finger on it.

NGOZI: We were all so used to mostly crappy conversation –

MAIKO: When that's all you could have, well –

GREG: Well, it took a while to sink in. I mean we really were used to talking shit most of the time.

NGOZI: Because crap was most of what there was, when crap became all there was it didn't become immediately apparent; you still went around for a while expecting to have a good conversation – I mean they had been scarce but they weren't extinct.

MAIKO: So we thought.

GREG: So we thought.

NGOZI: So we thought. Until, like, I don't know, two years or so into it people began to talk about how much of a waste of time talking had become and soon that's all people were talking about. And then we hit the streets demanding some kind of action – a study, a report, an inquiry, anything.

MAIKO: But we were stonewalled at every turn.

GREG: Every bureaucratic door that could get slammed in our faces got slammed in our faces.

NGOZI: Soon, people started to crash in-camera sessions at city council, delegates stormed the legislature, and we even sent a few representatives to the moon.

MAIKO: Nothing.

GREG: And that's when we dismantled almost everything in sight.

NGOZI: And threw the pieces hard, fast and without a single hesitation.

MAIKO: It was over before it had begun.

GREG: And now we speak deeply and we speak freely.

NGOZI: Or at least that's what it feels like.

MAIKO: If you feel free does that mean you are free?

NGOZI: What if you just don't know any better?

GREG: Do you feel free?

MAIKO: What does freedom feel like?

NGOZI: Well, I've experienced servitude and this doesn't feel like that.

GREG: Check your chest – is your heart free?

MAIKO: Um –

NGOZI: It doesn't feel free.

MAIKO: It feels trapped by the responsibility it has toward the blood.

NGOZI: My ribs are a cage.

MAIKO: What about our feet?

GREG: No, they can't just walk into traffic.

NGOZI: Or dog shit.

MAIKO: Do they know that?

GREG: Yes, most definitely.

NGOZI: I can feel they know that.

MAIKO: What about our hands?

GREG: Um, no, no. They possess the power to touch but only with permission.

NGOZI: Are our genitals free?

GREG/MAIKO: No.

GREG: What about our faces? Are they free?

NGOZI: They're free to smile.

MAIKO: Yeah.

GREG: That's true.

NGOZI: They're free to frown.

MAIKO: Yeah.

GREG: No problem there.

NGOZI: But are they free to do this? *(she makes a face)*

GREG: This? *(he makes a face)*

MAIKO: This? *(she makes a face)*

GREG: If our faces do that they'll probably get tossed in the nut house along with the rest of us.

NGOZI: So no.

MAIKO: Well, then, I don't feel free. Not a single solitary part of me.

GREG: That's frightening.

MAIKO: Is it?

GREG: I don't know.

(Sound of crickets begins again.)

NGOZI: Before the revolution fright was used as a means of social control.

GREG: Because frightened people listen to instructions.

MAIKO: But the frightened people can't feel like they're frightened.

GREG: No, they got to feel like they're free. At least a couple of times a day.

NGOZI: Before the revolution, fright masqueraded as short bursts of freedom which travelled the world and were fed into your brain every time you picked up the phone and said hello.

GREG: That's right, that's why cell phones were so popular.

MAIKO: They were also popular because popularity was popular.

NGOZI: The populace was always looking for new ways to be popular.

GREG: The cell phone fed popularity right into your ear canal like toothpaste from a tube.

MAIKO: Popularity itself or the illusion of popularity?

NGOZI: The illusion of popularity, I believe.

GREG: The sensation of popularity.

NGOZI: That's right, the sensation of popularity. As long as you felt you were popular then the track was greased with the fat of the land. It kept the wheels a-turnin'.

GREG: It certainly kept the nightclubs a-hoppin'.

MAIKO: I thought it was sex that kept the nightclubs a-hoppin'.

GREG: As I recall, sex and popularity were somehow related.

NGOZI: Before the revolution I used to feel horny every time I felt inadequate.

MAIKO: That doesn't make any sense.

GREG: No, I understand. The horniness was not a thing there, right, it was a thing missing. It was inadequacy made flesh.

NGOZI: That's exactly it.

MAIKO: Before the revolution I was very self-defecating.

GREG: Do you mean deprecating?

MAIKO: No, I mean I was always shitting on myself.

NGOZI: That was a popular pastime.

GREG: It was depressing.

MAIKO: I hated myself because the minute I tried to believe something, I learned something that would contradict it.

GREG: Most of my beliefs were arbitrarily acquired.

NGOZI: There were a few things that were certain.

MAIKO: The rich got richer and the poor got poorer.

NGOZI: But even saying that –

MAIKO: Too true – it was so obvious that saying it made me feel like I was saying the sky was blue. I mean, who but the most idiotic person would point that out?

GREG: The terrible things in the world managed to hide themselves by simply capitalizing on their obviousness.

NGOZI: Which was a profound contradiction.

MAIKO: Contradiction was everywhere.

GREG: It was the air we breathed.

NGOZI: The water we drank.

MAIKO: The food we ate.

GREG: I was so full of contradiction, I would sometimes introduce myself as somebody else.

NGOZI: Oh, I know, that was embarrassing.

GREG: Tell me about it.

MAIKO: How did you usually handle it?

GREG: I rolled my nose, stamped my eyes and clacked my feet together. The usual, I guess.

NGOZI: But there were some things you could really believe and say into a microphone, if need be.

MAIKO: True.

GREG: But trying to live your beliefs, well, that was tricky as hell.

NGOZI: And everyone knew it was tricky.

MAIKO: But we couldn't give each other a break.

NGOZI: My head seemed to be circling the planet like a blind bird on fire.

MAIKO: I try not to think about it but sometimes I'm stunned by the depths to which I would sink. When I was a waiter I took pleasure in informing people the kitchen had closed.

NGOZI: That's normal.

MAIKO: The city seemed like it was crawling with all sorts of people who felt entitled to all sorts of things.

GREG: Well, it was.

NGOZI: Still is.

GREG: Some say.

MAIKO: People came to expect the most fantastic things as if they were completely normal.

NGOZI: Like romance.

MAIKO: Romance seemed to be everywhere.

NGOZI: It was a frenzy.

GREG: And bank robberies.

MAIKO: Oh yeah.

NGOZI: I tried to rob a bank.

(Music: Quincy Jones's 'Money'; crickets fade.)

GREG: What happened?

NGOZI: The teller pulled a gun on me. She took all the money I had and my library card.

MAIKO: Did you cancel it?

NGOZI: I was going to until I found that the bank teller was taking out interesting books, reading them and somehow – don't ask me how – I was absorbing the information.

GREG: Knowledge with no work?

NGOZI: None.

MAIKO: Amazing.

NGOZI: I knew all these new things: how to build a kite, ways to make a relationship work, Chinese astrology, theories on radical democracy –

GREG: That must have come in handy.

NGOZI: – and the plots of novels I've never read.

MAIKO: What's she reading these days?

NGOZI: I think she's dead.

GREG: Maybe she just lost the card.

NGOZI: Maybe, but the last book she read was *Suicide For Dummies*.

MAIKO: Oh, that's a good book, believe it or not.

GREG: I believe it.

MAIKO: It tells you how to kill yourself so that no one would know.

NGOZI: I remember that.

GREG: How?

MAIKO: Well –

NGOZI: It had something to do with tricking the soul into thinking the body was already dead at which point it would just up and leave.

MAIKO: That was a good one because your empty body would wander around for the rest of its life and nobody would be the wiser.

NGOZI: It was in the chapter entitled 'Sparing Your Family the Misery.'

GREG: So you figure the bank teller is dead?

NGOZI: I'm pretty sure she's dead, but I have this feeling that without access to books she's found another hobby.

MAIKO: What is it?

NGOZI: Well, I sometimes wake up at night with a number in my head and I'll attempt to say it aloud but it's so large that it would probably take me a few days; it's my guess that since she died she's taken up counting to infinity.

GREG: That's entirely plausible.

NGOZI: I just hope it doesn't keep me up at night.

MAIKO: That could be annoying.

NGOZI: On the other hand, the implications of her reaching a final number and having to either stop or go backwards are chilling.

(Music out.)

GREG: That is chilling.

NGOZI: I think I would prefer her to keep going.

MAIKO: Do you want a sweater?

GREG: It's okay, I'll just rub my hands together.

NGOZI: Some days the world is cold.

MAIKO: It shivers the future and makes ice cubes out of the past.

NGOZI: It freezes my history into a landscape of lies.

GREG: But I'm not without a little guilt.

MAIKO: Oh, I'm guilty.

NGOZI: I've made mistakes.

GREG: But you know, since the revolution things have changed. You can't trust the things that seemed so straightforward and eternal. There's new things to trust.

NGOZI: True.

GREG: The trees have reversed their traditional pattern and instead of dropping their leaves in the fall they drop their branches, leaving the leaves to hover in the air.

MAIKO: That's how I felt about my relationships with my lovers. The branches just weren't there but something was keeping me from leaving.

GREG: Is that a pun?

MAIKO: It is.

NGOZI: You look classy when you pun.

MAIKO: That's too bad.

GREG: You know, I didn't know I was working class until someone handed me a shovel.

MAIKO: What did you do with it?

GREG: Well, I was so taken aback I simply hit them over the head with it.

NGOZI: Did you get in trouble?

GREG: I spent the night in jail. When I explained to the judge what had happened he was very understanding. He said that if someone had told him he was working class he might not have stopped with the shovel and congratulated me for my restraint.

MAIKO: So you got off?

GREG: He told me that if I felt like it I could take a box of peanut butter to a food bank.

NGOZI: Did you?

GREG: No, it was too much work.

L to R: Ngozi Paul, Assistant Director Troy O'Donnell, Maiko Bae Yamamoto

MAIKO: I worked in an office building before the revolution and developed Bell's palsy while sitting near the air conditioner.

GREG: What's Bell's palsy?

MAIKO: It's this nerve thing. The left side of my face became entirely slack, my mouth drooped, and my left eye always remained open – which was lucky because I was able to see the whole thing coming.

(Music: Eddie Harris's 'The Things You Do.')

NGOZI: Are people lonelier these days?

GREG: I know I am.

MAIKO: The isolating effects of critical thinking has been a development I hadn't anticipated.

NGOZI: Personally, I thought the opposite would be true.

MAIKO: I fell in love during the revolution.

GREG: How did that go?

MAIKO: Strangely, my lover had also developed Bell's palsy, but on the other side of their face, so when we made love, both of our open eyes would stare forlornly at each other, wishing desperately to close.

NGOZI: Sometimes privacy is important when you're making love.

GREG: You don't want your partner always staring at you.

NGOZI: It's unnerving.

MAIKO: It became our downfall; we saw each other too clearly.

GREG: Denial is the lifeblood of love, after all.

MAIKO: True.

NGOZI: And love is the lifeblood of life.

GREG: Yup.

NGOZI: Before the revolution we had holidays that tried to force us to celebrate love and life.

GREG: But since the revolution we instead celebrate the disappointment felt in response to the way love and life have simply not lived up to expectation.

NGOZI: I first thought that revelling in that disappointment would cause some kind of suicide epidemic.

GREG: I was surprised at the results myself.

MAIKO: Ironically, the Day of Disappointment has been the least disappointing aspect of my life here on earth.

NGOZI: How can you feel like things are not going according to schedule when disappointment is the only thing you're expected to feel?

GREG: On that day, no matter how things go, you're always entirely up to the task, completely competent.

MAIKO: Even if you aren't feeling like life and love are disappointing you, you can feel disappointment that on the day to celebrate disappointment you weren't disappointed.

NGOZI: Too much happiness always leads to sadness so the Day of Disappointment keep the populace on more of an even keel.

GREG: Too much sadness always seems to lead to silence.

MAIKO: Sometimes silence is not so bad.

NGOZI: No.

(They become silent for a long while. Eventually, the distant sound of crickets is heard.)

NGOZI: I can feel my hair growing.

GREG: I've never noticed that before.

MAIKO: I can see my vision fading.

GREG: Really?

MAIKO: The rods and cones in your retina make these tiny explosions when they die.

GREG: Oh yeah, wow, that's kind of beautiful.

MAIKO: It's like fireworks.

NGOZI: Hey, if you listen carefully you can hear the living hairs in your cochlea drying and tipping over.

MAIKO: It sounds like tiny trees falling in the forest.

GREG: I can feel the roots of my teeth turning to liquid.

MAIKO: Decay is actually very beautiful.

NGOZI: Too bad it smells so bad.

MAIKO: Chew gum.

GREG: Good idea.

(Gum suddenly materializes in their mouths. They blow the occasional bubble. They do a small piece of choreography and the Eddie Harris song is again re-established.)

GREG: Before the revolution the only way I could get to sleep was by thinking violent thoughts.

MAIKO: I floated to town one day on a stream of my own vomit.

NGOZI: Sometimes I was in a good mood.

MAIKO: These good moods –

NGOZI: What about them?

MAIKO: Well, if I recall correctly, they were owned by a selected group and were rented out on occasion.

NGOZI: Yes.

GREG: During the revolution I remember a mechanical rotation of good moods based on a disk that went whipping through the air.

MAIKO: I remember that crazy thing.

GREG: It nearly clipped my head off once.

NGOZI: I was really broke and when I needed a haircut I would wait and as it flew by I would step outside.

GREG: I did the same when I started getting a little long in the tooth.

MAIKO: But my good moods were always interrupted by guilt.

NGOZI: Guilt of what?

MAIKO: That I had made a mistake.

GREG: Had you?

MAIKO: Of course. How are you supposed to acquire the knowledge yielded by making a mistake without making the mistake?

NGOZI: You can't.

GREG: I've heard that's one of life's Sixty-six Sexy Secrets.

NGOZI: I mean, having someone describe the peril of the mistake is almost never enough to dissuade most from having to make the same mistake themselves.

MAIKO: Well, the knowledge yielded is often so subtle.

GREG: Unless we're talking about the implications of jumping off a cliff.

MAIKO: No, you're right, there are some dangers easily explained.

NGOZI: Putting your hand on a hot stove.

GREG: Falling in love with your mother.

NGOZI: But most of life's mistakes are not so cut and dried.

MAIKO: Most of life's mistakes come as certain and sudden surprises.

NGOZI: I mean, would I make the mistake if I thought it was a mistake?

GREG: Of course not.

NGOZI: So, the life knowledge that is lacking to understand that it is a mistake is happily offered by making the mistake.

MAIKO: It's an elegant system.

GREG: So simple.

NGOZI: So, why feel guilty when making a mistake?

GREG: That's a good question.

MAIKO: Let's just forget about the revolution for a second –

(Music and crickets snap out.)

NGOZI: Okay.

MAIKO: And talk about a few things that have become commonplace in our new lives.

GREG: Shadow puppetry.

NGOZI: Or shadow boxing.

GREG: Both.

MAIKO: The sadness of the skies.

NGOZI: That's just rain.

MAIKO: Is it?

NGOZI: I think so.

GREG: I do one thing a week that will benefit someone less fortunate than I.

NGOZI: Me too.

MAIKO: Me too.

GREG: And I receive some weekly crumb of support from someone more fortunate than I.

NGOZI: Me too.

MAIKO: Me too.

NGOZI: I feel my body fully.

MAIKO: That's a nice one.

NGOZI: Before the revolution I was feeling my body less and less.

GREG: I used to feel like my hands had been cut off by some magical scythe. It was right before the revolution and I was at some kind of an event that required clapping.

MAIKO: What was clapping all about?

NGOZI: Yes, that one was strange.

GREG: And at the moment when slapping my hands together again and again and again was considered absolutely the thing to do –

MAIKO: When to not do it would have been rude?

GREG: At that moment I just couldn't do it.

NGOZI: Was the event bad?

GREG: It just felt like my hands had disappeared and that all I could slap together was the idea of my hands.

MAIKO: So what did you do?

GREG: Nothing. I just sat there and caused a bit of a stir.

NGOZI: I read about you in the papers.

GREG: That was kind of a stupid article.

NGOZI: True.

MAIKO: I never understood the point of clapping.

NGOZI: I think it was vestigial.

MAIKO: What did it do?

NGOZI: I think it was just a way of saying thank you.

GREG: I think it was more about showing some kind of approval.

MAIKO: So was it a social construction?

NGOZI: I think it was.

GREG: It wasn't like a kiss you could feel sizzling down to your groin.

NGOZI: No, it wasn't like being kissed.

MAIKO: But it might have had a direct physical effect.

GREG: Maybe.

NGOZI: I don't know.

MAIKO: I think we should try.

GREG: Really?

MAIKO: Sure.

GREG: Okay, I guess.

NGOZI: It might be interesting.

MAIKO: Okay. On three. One, two, three.

(They clap for a while.)

MAIKO: Is it doing anything?

GREG: I don't know.

(More clapping.)

NGOZI: It doesn't seem like it.

(More clapping.)

MAIKO: Try it louder.

(They clap louder.)

GREG: Anything?

NGOZI: My hands are getting sore.

MAIKO: Let's clap for each other.

GREG: Okay, you first.

(Maiko stops clapping.)

NGOZI: How does that feel?

GREG: Do you feel good about yourself?

NGOZI: Do you feel like we approve of you?

MAIKO: I don't know.

GREG: Do you feel like bowing?

MAIKO: Not really.

NGOZI: Try to bow and see if anything falls into place.

MAIKO: Okay, but – *(she bows)* No, I don't understand this bowing. It makes even less sense than the clapping.

GREG: Let me try.

(Maiko claps. Greg stops clapping and starts bowing.)

MAIKO: Well?

GREG: I have no idea what I'm trying to communicate with this crazy manoeuvre.

NGOZI: I guess you're trying to say, 'Thank you and I accept your approval.'

GREG: It's ridiculous.

NGOZI: May I try?

GREG: Go ahead.

(Greg claps again. Ngozi stops clapping and starts bowing. The sound of a massive audience applauding rises. Ngozi gets carried away.)

NGOZI: Thank you. Thank you. Thank you.

(The sound of applause fades.)

MAIKO: Wow.

GREG: Everybody okay?

NGOZI: That was crazy.

GREG: My hands are all tingly.

MAIKO: Yeah.

GREG: Look, my life line has doubled.

NGOZI: I guess clapping is good for you.

MAIKO: Maybe approving of others can clear space for yourself.

NGOZI: But my life line has scattered.

MAIKO: Maybe approving of others can take space away.

GREG: Maybe approving of others should proceed with caution.

MAIKO: Hey. All my lines have shifted to spell 'Don't drop the ball.'

NGOZI: What ball?

MAIKO: I've never owned a ball.

GREG: It's probably a wrong number.

MAIKO: Clapping and bowing. Wow. They really need to be seen to be believed.

GREG: They do almost defy description.

NGOZI: You know, I've always wanted to defy description; I think that would be fabulous.

MAIKO: I guess.

GREG: Yeah, it's hard to know.

NGOZI: It is hard to know. But if I could just try it just once. Just to see what it would be like. Just once. I think that would be enough.

GREG: It's probably exactly like everything else.

MAIKO: Really? But I don't like to believe that all moments, things and thoughts are equally valid.

NGOZI: No.

Darren O'Donnell and murr (right)

GREG: I suppose it comes down to how you feel about them.

MAIKO: Is this moment, for example, more valid than this one?

NGOZI: If I gave you a kiss in the middle of it, you might feel it a bit more.

MAIKO: That's true.

GREG: Or if the ground opened up and swallowed us.

MAIKO: That would be a moment to remember.

NGOZI: Or never forget.

MAIKO: Or never forget.

GREG: The unforgettable moment has more reality. It's still here, still hanging on. The moments you forget, well, forget about them, but the ones you can't forget; you can build buildings on them.

NGOZI: Cities.

MAIKO: Nations.

GREG: Empires.

NGOZI: Still, there's something about being forgettable that I really like.

MAIKO: Hard to make money off it.

GREG: It sure is.

NGOZI: I sometimes feel like everything is pulling me toward forgetting.

GREG: Remember and you're doomed to either do or not do what you've always done.

NGOZI: True.

GREG: Forget and you're finished.

MAIKO: Remember and all the bricks in the walls will hug you and may never let you go.

GREG: Forget and one day you might be walking down the street and you'll find you can walk through walls.

MAIKO: You can walk through people.

GREG: They can walk through you.

MAIKO: Forget and you're free – invisible but free.

GREG: Remember and you'll be forever watched, even if only by yourself.

NGOZI: I dodge through remembering and forgetting like a child playing in a field covered in landmines. It feels like my little legs have been blown off but I look down and there they are keeping me stuck to the terrible ground.

MAIKO: Would you rather float away?

NGOZI: I'm just afraid I wouldn't be able to recognize the difference.

GREG: That's the thing.

NGOZI: Hey.

MAIKO: What?

NGOZI: Am I turning into a pipsqueak?

MAIKO: What?

GREG: No, you're okay.

NGOZI: Are you sure?

GREG: No, no, I know, I used to run a daycare for pipsqueaks.

MAIKO: Really?

GREG: You're okay.

MAIKO: How was that?

GREG: It was sort of fun; they were always running around trying to lick their own bums.

NGOZI: Oh, I've never wanted to do that.

GREG: See, you're fine.

MAIKO: The few pipsqueaks I've met were only ever able to talk about their careers.

GREG: Yeah, you'd ask them what was up and they'd pretty much recite recent additions to their resume.

MAIKO: Have you ever seen a pipsqueak get caught in the machinery?

NGOZI: Oh, that's awful.

MAIKO: I couldn't have imagined such blood.

NGOZI: And the screams.

GREG: Once I was sitting lost in thought and from quite a distance came this sound, and without really paying attention to it, somewhere in the back of my mind, I thought someone was singing.

MAIKO: But it was a dying pipsqueak?

NGOZI: Sometimes I really feel like I'm turning into one.

MAIKO: Even if you were, they can reverse the process.

NGOZI: How?

GREG: But you're not.

MAIKO: Some radiation thing.

GREG: I read this article about aging.

MAIKO: Uh huh?

GREG: It said that they've discovered the gene responsible and that they know how to remove it.

MAIKO: Oh, I heard about that. They bathe you in some kind of radiation or something.

NGOZI: Same kind as with pipsqueaks?

MAIKO: No, no, different.

GREG: I heard that they can radiate select parts of the body and only those would remain young.

MAIKO: The big fear is that it's going to be used to create armies of children.

GREG: And legions of child prostitutes.

NGOZI: Really?

GREG: I've heard an island for that very purpose has been set up.

MAIKO: Imagine that.

GREG: It's going to be somewhere in the tropics.

NGOZI: Of course.

GREG: There will vacation packages.

MAIKO: Those who can afford it will spend weeks there.

NGOZI: That makes me sick.

GREG: You've got to wonder if some of those people actually possess souls.

MAIKO: Come to think of it, they might not.

NGOZI: You don't think?

MAIKO: Well, there's this other thing I read back when they proved the soul was an eternal energy. Did you read about it?

GREG: I'm not sure.

MAIKO: It was some kind of thing, a device or something, that was able to tap and use that power.

NGOZI: Really?

MAIKO: It was a tiny article and I haven't heard about it since.

GREG: Did it say how it worked?

MAIKO: It just said that the soul of one mouse could power a flashlight.

NGOZI: Forever?

MAIKO: Apparently for eternity. It made the paper because the head of the research team had been refused access to human souls, so she had killed herself in order to continue the research.

GREG: But I thought that if you kill yourself you can't dictate the use of your soul.

MAIKO: Well, exactly – it was a big legal wrangle.

NGOZI: I hope she had a good lawyer.

MAIKO: Anyway, it puts me in mind of that new generating station.

GREG: What about it?

MAIKO: Well, it doesn't burn coal, it's not nuclear, it's not wind or water ...

NGOZI: Do you think – ?

GREG: They said it had something to do with the power of speech.

MAIKO: They say whatever they want.

NGOZI: You think it's the souls of millions of pedophiles?

MAIKO: Could be the souls of anyone. Including us.

GREG: Wouldn't we know?

MAIKO: I don't know.

NGOZI: Losing your soul must feel like something.

MAIKO: Maybe not.

GREG: You don't think there would be a pang?

NGOZI: Of regret?

GREG: Of something.

MAIKO: Well, without a soul, what would be left to feel it?

GREG: Can we talk about something else?

NGOZI: If my soul was being used to generate power for the people I would want a cut.

MAIKO: Before the revolution I thought I was responsible for solving the world's problems.

GREG: I have this feeling that I'm going to grow very old.

MAIKO: I have this feeling that I already am.

NGOZI: I know.

GREG: I know.

MAIKO: Real old.

NGOZI: I know.

GREG: I know.

(There is a ringing sound. Greg lifts his hand to look at it. It holds a cell phone.)

GREG: Hello? Really? Wow. Really. Really? Really. Okay. Love you. Bye.

(Greg turns off the cell phone and lowers his hand.)

NGOZI: What?

GREG: Creatures have been spotted.

MAIKO: Again?!

NGOZI: What kind are they?

GREG: They're ugly, apparently.

MAIKO: Of course they're ugly.

NGOZI: They're always ugly.

MAIKO: I always get suicidal whenever those things are around.

GREG: I've heard they peck away at the grounding components of one's sense of self.

NGOZI: I know.

GREG: And then pull it right out of your nose.

MAIKO: It's supposed to feel terrible.

NGOZI: How do they know that?

MAIKO: How do they know drowning feels nice?

GREG: Have you ever heard a creature eat a pipsqueak? That is something else.

NGOZI: Really?

GREG: It sounds a lot like the unrealizable potential of the future impaling itself on the rigidity of the past.

NGOZI: Oh no, that's an awful sound.

MAIKO: Oh yeah, that's because in the past I was pretty much an idiot.

GREG: Me, too.

NGOZI: Me, too.

MAIKO: I look back on my life and I have to admit that most of my thinking was a mess; it was completely uninformed by things I've learned in the years since.

NGOZI: Living certainly has informed how I live my life.

MAIKO: And without everything I've learned, the kind of person I was could be described as an idiot.

NGOZI: Described as an idiot, I was a total idiot.

GREG: Wait a second. If that's true –

NGOZI: Oh, it's true all right.

GREG: Well, in a number of years what will happen when we look back on this moment – these things we are thinking, these words we are saying, these people we are?

NGOZI: Well, with all the new information gathered we'll realize that ... oh.

GREG: Exactly.

MAIKO: So right now – ?

NGOZI: Right now ...

GREG: Right now ... I must be an idiot.

MAIKO: Yes.

GREG: A fucking total idiot.

NGOZI: That makes two of us.

MAIKO: Make that three.

GREG: I have never thought like this before.

NGOZI: It's a massive piece of information.

GREG: I'm an idiot.

NGOZI: I'm an idiot.

MAIKO: I'm an idiot.

GREG: I'm an idiot.

MAIKO: I'm an idiot.

NGOZI: I'm an idiot.

MAIKO: I'm an idiot.

GREG: I'm an idiot.

NGOZI: I'm an idiot.

GREG: I'm an idiot.

MAIKO: I'm an idiot.

GREG: I'm an idiot.

MAIKO: I'm an idiot.

NGOZI: I'm an idiot.

GREG: I'm an idiot.

NGOZI: I'm an idiot.

MAIKO: I'm an idiot.

NGOZI: I'm an idiot.

GREG: I'm an idiot.

NGOZI: I'm an idiot.

MAIKO: I'm an idiot.

GREG: I'm an idiot.

(The theatre shudders, the lights flicker, there's the sound of distant rumbling and then the whole thing shuts down; the emergency lights click on, casting a pale glow onto the audience and the stage. There is silence. Nobody moves. A few seconds pass. A cell phone rings. The theatre starts up again with a whining or grinding sound, the lights come on, and Greg lifts his hand, looks at it like he's not sure what is going on, then recognizes that it is holding a cell phone, which he answers.)

GREG. Hello? No, I'm sorry, you must have the wrong number. That's okay. Bye.

MAIKO: Whew. *(she lifts a cigarette)* I need a smoke. Do you mind?

GREG: No. I could do with a drag myself.

NGOZI: Can I bum one?

(They move upstage, stepping into and onto the spandex, which gives way to reveal a riser. They sit on it.)

MAIKO: They're clove.

NGOZI: Oh, that's all right, then.

MAIKO: You can have one.

GREG: I just want a drag.

NGOZI: Oh maybe I'll try it. Can I have a drag?

MAIKO: Sure, they're good for you. Do you have a light?

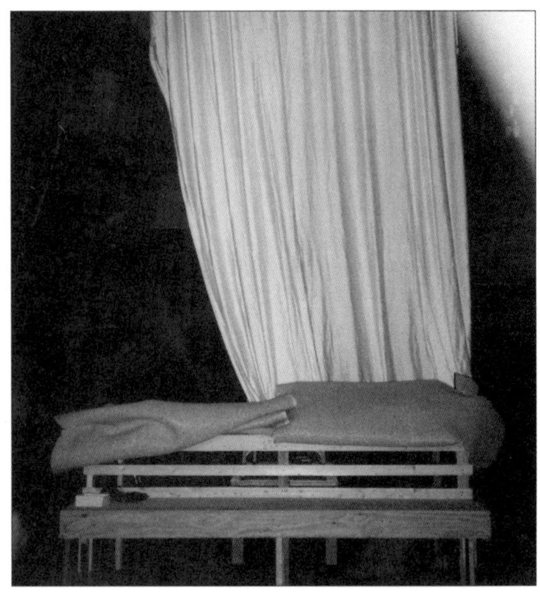

GREG: Here.

(He lifts his hand, which holds a lighter, and lights it for her. They pass the smoke around. Long silence.)

GREG: Smells like pumpkin pie.

MAIKO: It's clove.

NGOZI: Pumpkin seeds are good for dealing with intestinal worms.

GREG: And unwanted astral entities.

MAIKO: I'm told that's why we have them out at Halloween.

GREG: I once saw a man chain-smoke fifty cigarettes.

MAIKO: Two packs?

GREG: Yeah.

NGOZI: Yuck.

GREG: Yeah. *(pause)* Something about it made me cry.

MAIKO: Are you sure it wasn't just the smoke getting in your eyes?

GREG: No, no, I wept like a child.

NGOZI: Nice.

GREG: Yeah. At one point everything disappeared except for the crying.

MAIKO: All you were was crying?

GREG: No ... more like ... all there was – and ever had been – was crying.

(They pause for a moment, then all sing together a few lines from Hoagy Carmichael's 'When Love Goes Wrong.' A star falls from the sky.)

ALL: It's like we said
You're better off dead
When love has lost its glow
So take this down
In black and white
When love goes wrong
Nothing goes right.

(Music: Soft Machine's 'Carol Ann.')

NGOZI: I don't feel very stable.

MAIKO: Is that a new feeling?

NGOZI: I've felt it for a few years.

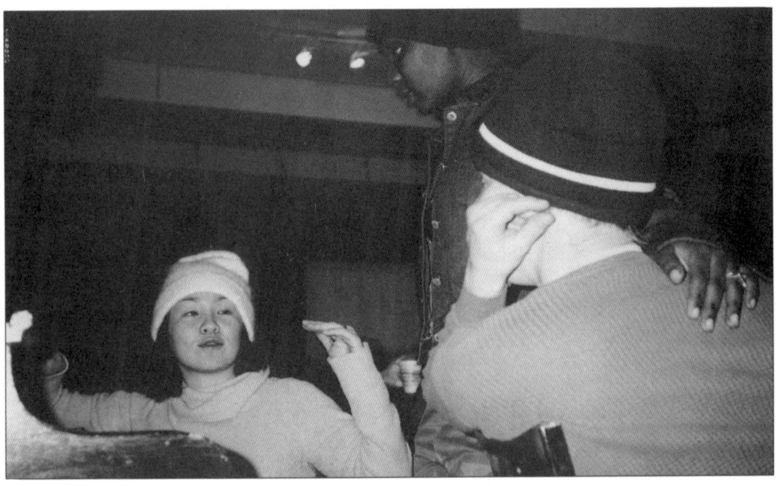

GREG: Did something happen?

NGOZI: I dunno, sort of. Who knows? I blame it on that rotten romance.

GREG: Have you been in a relationship since?

NGOZI: No.

MAIKO: What do you do with all your time?

NGOZI: Well, to occupy the hours I would have spent with my beloved making love or lying in bed and talking about our childhood, our fears, our hopes – you know, just carving out of the thick hot air of empty space the person we thought we'd always wanted to be for the benefit of the person we thought we'd be best with – to occupy those long empty hours I took a course in shorthand and became somewhat of an amateur stenographer.

MAIKO: Nice.

NGOZI: I would sit for hours, notating what was happening. You know, like, what was being said, who said it, how it was said, and to whom it was addressed.

GREG: Nice.

MAIKO: What if you were alone?

NGOZI: I started keeping a constant written track of everything I thought.

GREG: Wow.

NGOZI: I noticed that the thoughts could be grouped according to different general patterns. I gave the patterns names and soon it turned into yet another conversation. Then I started to look for traces of the gods in the conversations.

GREG: Were traces there?

NGOZI: Just small things at first. Words only. The first one was, if I recall correctly: Sandwich.

MAIKO: That was the gods' first word to you?

GREG: What kind of sandwich?

MAIKO: Was it a request? A command?

GREG: Were you being mistaken for a waitress?

NGOZI: No, no mistake, I was a waitress.

GREG: So, did you get the gods a sandwich?

NGOZI: Well, I decided not to take the order literally since I was working as a waitress in a cocktail bar. I mean, we just didn't serve sandwiches.

MAIKO: What did you do?

NGOZI: I brought the gods an idea sandwiched between two other ideas.

GREG: Mmmm, that sounds good.

MAIKO: What were the ideas?

NGOZI: I simply envisioned a world where coincidence had become entirely normal and not particularly mystical. I mean, it was mystical; it just wasn't a harbinger of something unusual suddenly happening because something unusual was always happening – so much so that it was completely usual, the norm. But the thing was, nothing appeared to be changing. In fact, it was getting worse along the same lines.

MAIKO: So coincidence was everywhere?

NGOZI: Yeah.

MAIKO: And usually things were unusual?

NGOZI: Yeah.

MAIKO: Yet things always remained the same?

NGOZI: Or got worse along the same lines.

GREG: So, I guess that was the meat in your sandwich.

NGOZI: Exactly.

MAIKO: And the slices of bread?

NGOZI: Well, they had to be light, airy, but fibrous – wholesome.

GREG: So, what were they?

NGOZI: One slice was that for coincidence to actually make some difference in a world riddled with coincidence, the populace would have to learn to love each other in a new way – a super way, an incredible way, a way totally unheard of.

GREG: How?

NGOZI: I haven't a clue. Love would just have to operate with some new premise. A premise as of yet – and perhaps forever – totally unknown.

MAIKO: And what's the other slice?

NGOZI: That the gods would either have to shit or get off the pot.

GREG: Is it the gods that are still on the pot?

NGOZI: Someone's constipated.

MAIKO: So, did they like the sandwich?

NGOZI: They never got back to me.

GREG: They never do.

NGOZI: All this chit-chat about that sandwich has made me hungry.

GREG: Yeah, I'd love some dweebs.

MAIKO: I have a fortune cookie.

NGOZI: That might hit the spot. Thanks.

(Ngozi breaks open the cookie.)

MAIKO: What's it say?

NGOZI: It's too dark.

GREG: I have a light.

NGOZI: Here.

GREG: Well, it says, 'Listen, Idiots, if you want Love to be anything more than comfort for cold nights, or an inclination to find yourself part of the thingamajig that always sits excellent and exclusive of you, or a panicked disavowal of the vicissitudes of constant solitude; if Love is to realize its revolutionary potential, its ability to alter the very terms of the agreement, its status as something you do for reasons you don't know because reason –'

MAIKO: We all understand the limits of reason.

NGOZI: Yeah, skip that part.

GREG: ' – if Love is going to be anything more than a Microphone Check, a Placing of the Inside Out, an Accidental Fostering of Temporary Allegiances for the Purposes of Self-Propulsion – '

MAIKO: Not to mention a good place to get laid.

GREG: ' – then Love is going to have to make do with less. Much, much less. In fact, if the truth be known, Love is going to have to make do with nothing, with no one, not even yourself.'

(The Soft Machine song fades.)

NGOZI: Huh.

GREG: I wonder what that means.

MAIKO: Does it come with any lucky lotto numbers?

GREG: It does: 41, 65, 16, 01, and the bonus number is 29. Hey, those numbers sound familiar.

MAIKO: They're the lucky numbers I always use –

GREG: Me too!

NGOZI: Wait a sec –

MAIKO: And I've never won a thing.

GREG: Me neither!

NGOZI: Say them again.

GREG: 41, 65, 16, 01 and 29.

NGOZI: Hey, that's my freaking phone number!

GREG: Really?

NGOZI: This is bizarre.

MAIKO: This is crazy.

GREG: This is creepy.

NGOZI: Whatever – coincidences are a dime a dozen.

GREG: I guess.

MAIKO: And things haven't changed that much.

NGOZI: Exactly.

GREG: *(springing to his feet)* Hey! I just realized I'm in love.

MAIKO: Really?

NGOZI: With who?

GREG: Nobody.

MAIKO: How does that feel?

GREG: Honestly, it feels pretty good. It feels kind of like a snowmobile suit.

NGOZI: Sweet.

(Greg yawns hugely.)

MAIKO: Are you okay?

GREG: I'm really tired.

NGOZI: Why don't you crash for a bit?

GREG: *(yawns again)* I think I will.

NGOZI: Good night.

GREG: Sweet dreams.

(Greg and Ngozi kiss.)

MAIKO: Good night.

GREG: Don't let the bedbugs bite.

(Greg and Maiko kiss. Greg retreats around behind the spandex. The intro to 'Sleep' by This Heat plays and we see Greg's shadow as he stretches and readies himself for bed. We also see the shadow of a thick duvet and fluffy pillows which he plumps. Ngozi and Maiko watch. Greg's shadow fades. Crickets fade in.)

MAIKO: I love that guy.

NGOZI: He's a really great guy.

MAIKO: Sometimes I feel so filled by this life.

NGOZI: It's a great feeling.

MAIKO: It is.

NGOZI: I love you.

MAIKO: Thanks. So do I. Sometimes. Sometimes I hate me.

NGOZI: Yeah.

MAIKO: Do you sometimes hate me, too?

NGOZI: Yeah.

MAIKO: That's okay, right?

NGOZI: It's okay with me.

MAIKO: Okay.

NGOZI: Actually, there was one person I loved without hating.

MAIKO: How was that?

NGOZI: It was hard. I don't think they were real.

MAIKO: Could you see them?

NGOZI: No, no, I never saw them.

MAIKO: Maybe they weren't real.

NGOZI: They sure felt real. It was before the revolution. I would be walking around, minding my own business, and then suddenly I would be filled with this intense happiness. I would sob.

MAIKO: You cried?

NGOZI: The crying slammed its way into my body and would crystallize around the need to phone my lover.

MAIKO: The lover you kicked out into the night?

NGOZI: No, I didn't have a lover at the time.

MAIKO: Well, then –

NGOZI: I know, it just felt like there was somebody there; I knew the kinds of times we had had together, I knew the kinds of jokes they liked, I even had a very strong sense of what it was like to make love to them.

MAIKO: But they didn't exist?

NGOZI: I could feel the contours of our personalities as they shaped themselves to fit each other. They were a substantial presence in my life – as substantial as many people who I know and have confirmed exist.

MAIKO: And love was the only thing you felt for them?

NGOZI: Never having met them, how could I feel anything but love?

MAIKO: Did you make gifts for them?

NGOZI: I wrote songs dedicated to them. Would you like me to sing one to you?

MAIKO: No.

NGOZI: It was a very odd way to spend my time.

MAIKO: We did have the most interesting ways of finding purpose. Myself, I became a DJ.

NGOZI: Did it give you a sense of purpose?

MAIKO: Well, it gave me something to do.

NGOZI: What's the difference between 'a purpose' and 'something to do'?

MAIKO: What's the difference between 'a purpose' and 'something to do'?

NGOZI: Yeah.

MAIKO: Should we just let that question hang?

NGOZI: Or float.

MAIKO: Will it hang or float?

NGOZI: Well, my sense is that a question like that has the potential to float.

MAIKO: Float away?

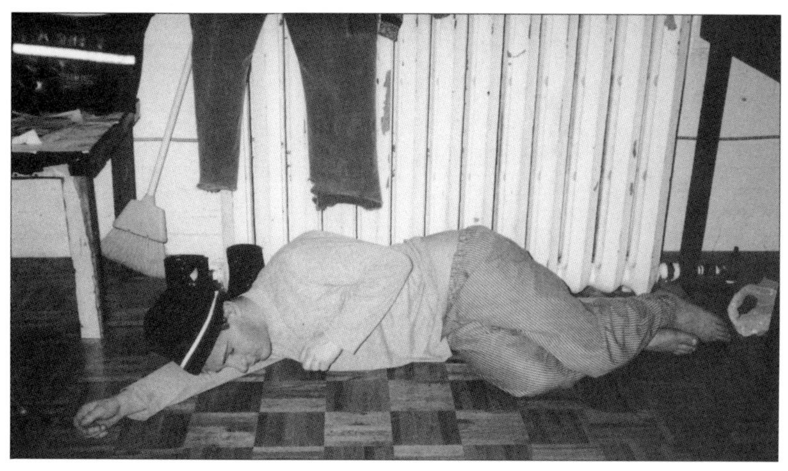

NGOZI: Around the corner and out the door like a feather on a sudden gust of wind blowing off the vast ocean of our muddled consciousness.

MAIKO: We should hang it.

NGOZI: Should we?

MAIKO: Hang it?

NGOZI: Hang it.

MAIKO: What is the difference between 'a purpose' and 'something to do'?

(They let the question hang. There is the sound of a siren in the distance.)

NGOZI: Well hung.

MAIKO: Thanks. Wow. Oh, that was intense. Wow.

NGOZI: Nice job.

MAIKO: Uh, um, whoa, I'm wiped out.

NGOZI: You did it really well.

MAIKO: Yeah?

NGOZI: Seriously.

MAIKO: Well, it almost fucking killed me.

NGOZI: Are you okay?

MAIKO: Yeah, I'll be fine. Um, so, what was I saying?

NGOZI: 'Purpose' and 'something to do.'

MAIKO: Oh yeah, uh, well, what occurred to me was that something to do can be a purpose, so in some ways there is no difference, but on the other hand, a purpose isn't necessarily something to do.

NGOZI: *(whistles)* Wow.

MAIKO: I know. I am just bagged.

NGOZI: Do you want to lie down?

MAIKO: I actually would.

NGOZI: Do your best.

MAIKO: You'll be okay by yourself?

NGOZI: I love being alone.

MAIKO: Sweet dreams.

NGOZI: Goodnight.

(They kiss. 'Sleep' by This Heat resumes. Maiko steps behind the spandex and we see her silhouette as she stretches and gets comfy. Greg is no longer there. Ngozi stands watching Maiko's shadow. Maiko settles down and the backlight fades. As the music continues to play Ngozi starts to become aware of the presence of someone. She slowly shifts and moves downstage. Music continues to play.)

NGOZI: Hello? Is anybody there? Hello? Anybody? Hello?

(Greg is discovered upstage right as the music finishes.)

GREG: Who are you talking to?

NGOZI: Oh, I didn't know you were awake.

(Greg moves downstage.)

GREG: Yeah, I'm awake. Who were you talking to?

NGOZI: I was just checking to see if anybody was there.

GREG: What made you think somebody might be there?

NGOZI: Nothing. I just didn't feel alone for a second.

GREG: You're not alone. I'm here.

NGOZI: I'm glad you're here.

GREG: I'm glad I'm here, too.

NGOZI: You're a great person, you know.

GREG: Thanks.

NGOZI: I'm glad you're in my life.

GREG: I love you.

NGOZI: Thank you. So do I. Sometimes. Sometimes I hate me.

GREG: Yeah.

NGOZI: Do you sometimes hate me, too?

GREG: Yeah.

NGOZI: That's okay, right?

GREG: It's okay with me.

NGOZI: Okay.

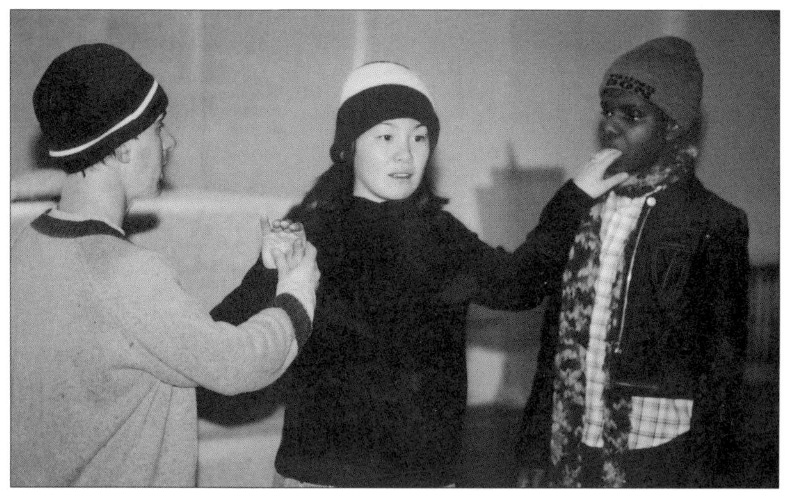

GREG: There was one person I loved without hating.

(The backlight fades up and we see Maiko's sleeping silhouette.)

NGOZI: How was that?

GREG: It was hard. I don't think they were real.

(Maiko's silhouette remains while Maiko herself is revealed to be standing just upstage left.)

NGOZI: Could you see them?

GREG: No, no, I never saw them.

NGOZI: Maybe they weren't real.

GREG: They sure felt real. It was before the revolution. I would be walking around minding my own business when I would be filled with this intense happiness; tears flowed out of my eyes.

(During the dialogue, Maiko moves downstage, between Greg and Ngozi. They don't see her. She looks at them, then plays a bit with their faces, sticking her fingers in their mouths, pulling out their cheeks, squashing their noses; all the while, they continue talking as if nothing is going on, their words distorted by all of Maiko's explorations.)

NGOZI: You cried?

GREG: The sobbing slammed its way into my body and would crystallize around the desire to phone my lover.

NGOZI: Which lover?

GREG: I didn't have a lover at the time.

NGOZI: Well, then –

GREG: It felt like there was somebody there, though; I knew the kinds of times we had had together, I knew the kinds of jokes

they liked, I even had a very strong sense of what it was like to make love to them.

NGOZI: But they didn't exist?

GREG: I could feel the contours of their personality as it shaped itself to fit mine. They were a substantial presence in my life – as substantial as many people who I know and have confirmed exist.

(Maiko finishes playing with their faces and walks upstage into the spandex and onto the platform, then ascends the ladder. When she reaches the top, high in the air above the stage, she goes to sleep. Her sleeping silhouette is illuminated down below.)

NGOZI: And love was the only thing you felt for them?

GREG: Never having met them, how could I feel anything but love?

NGOZI: Did you make gifts for them?

GREG: I wrote songs dedicated to them. Would you like me to sing one to you?

NGOZI: No.

(Maiko bolts awake. The sleeping silhouette is gone.)

MAIKO: Oh my gods!

(Greg and Ngozi move quickly onto the platform and up the ladder. They all cling together high in the air.)

NGOZI: It's okay.

MAIKO: Oh my gods!

GREG: You're all right. You're okay.

MAIKO: Oh my gods.

NGOZI: It's okay, it's okay.

MAIKO: I just had the most terrifying dream.

NGOZI: It's okay.

MAIKO: In the dream I was with you two and you were you, you were familiar, you were my friends, and then suddenly we had forgotten who we were to each other. And I said, 'Do you think we're friends?' And you said:

GREG: I think we're friends.

MAIKO: And I said, 'Do we like being friends?' And you said:

NGOZI: I guess we must.

MAIKO: Then I said, 'Will we ever not be friends?' And you said:

GREG: One day, I will be gone.

MAIKO: And then you said:

NGOZI: Nothing lasts forever. Ever.

MAIKO: And then all the flesh fell from our faces and our laughing teeth chattered in their skulls with nothing at all to keep time, not even the clicking of our hearts.

NGOZI: I can see why you were terrified.

Front: Choreographer Sarah Chase
Rear: Greg MacArthur, Ngozi Paul, Maiko Bae Yamamoto

GREG: The truth is frightening.

MAIKO: Hey, look, the sun's going to rise.

(Music: Ramsey Lewis's 'People Make the World Go Round' and the sound of birds.)

NGOZI: Oh, beautiful.

GREG: Wow!

MAIKO: That's really beautiful.

NGOZI: That's really bright.

MAIKO: It's making me feel better.

GREG: Melts the demons away.

(They begin to climb down the ladder, onto the platform and then onto the stage. They resume their positions across the front of the stage. They dance.)

NGOZI: Is it dangerous to stare at the rising sun?

MAIKO: It doesn't hurt.

GREG: It puts me in a good mood.

NGOZI: Whenever I'm in a good mood I become sad because I know that my mood will soon turn and soon I'll be depressed again.

GREG: How do you feel when you're depressed?

NGOZI: I feel happy to know that soon I'll be happy.

GREG: When I'm single I'm always excited, because I know soon I will be in love.

NGOZI: How do you feel when you're in love?

GREG: I feel sad to know that soon I'll be single and lonely.

MAIKO: Just like for me it's hard to enjoy sleeping because, soon, I know, I'll be awake.

GREG: And when you're awake?

MAIKO: Life is good, because before you know it – it's bedtime.

NGOZI: Life is bearable.

GREG: For now.

MAIKO: What are we going to do but enjoy now?

NGOZI: Or do our best to enjoy now.

GREG: Yes, or do our best to enjoy now.

MAIKO: Soon, now will go wrong like now always goes wrong.

NGOZI: I just wish there was some early warning signal.

GREG: The last time I noticed things were going wrong was when I noticed that the people I considered to be my friends had bad taste and the people with good taste considered my taste to be bad.

MAIKO: Did they consider you a friend?

GREG: They never returned my calls.

MAIKO: I had a lover once who had much better taste than me. I tried to keep up but ended up on the wrong side of style.

NGOZI: That must have been annoying.

MAIKO: It was terrifying, actually. The big realization was that while I cared I just didn't want to care.

GREG: That's a difficult impasse.

NGOZI: Couldn't you just let go and care?

MAIKO: I really didn't want to. I knew that caring was just about wanting to hear the bells on the big buildings ring every time I thought about myself. And, frankly, I couldn't give a shit about the big buildings, the bells, myself or the clocks that kept us all in line.

GREG: Style is time-based.

NGOZI: What about timeless classics?

GREG: Like what?

MAIKO: The wheel.

GREG: Okay.

NGOZI: I think the light bulb will have serious staying power.

MAIKO: I think the habit many people have when encountering a stranger in, say, a grocery store or on the street somewhere –

GREG: Which habit?

MAIKO: Of making eye contact, looking away and then smiling –

NGOZI: Yes.

MAIKO: I think that's something that will stay in fashion no matter what the designers of social apparel turn out.

GREG: It is truly a classic.

MAIKO: I use it almost daily.

GREG: That little tight smile that I paste on my face after averting my gaze simply assures me that I am a nice person, living in a nice place, surrounded by nice people, without having to actually expend any effort, without breaking a sweat, without taking what everybody says you should take but nobody ever does.

NGOZI: Which is – ?

GREG: Well, of course I'm speaking about what's known as – and here I'm going to use my fingers to indicate quotation marks –

MAIKO: Another timeless classic.

GREG: 'A risk.'

NGOZI: Risks are risky and best left to people who are looking forward to dying.

GREG: They're a rare breed.

NGOZI: Oddly enough.

MAIKO: I think it's because – what does everyone say? –

GREG: 'Death is a mystery.'

MAIKO: Death is a mystery.

NGOZI: What mystery? It's as common as life.

GREG: I consider life to be a mystery.

NGOZI: Maybe, okay, sometimes I do, but then I smell the armpit, it needs to be washed and I wash it. In the details there is no mystery.

MAIKO: No, that's true – in the details, life is obvious.

NGOZI: You hit the thumb with a hammer, the thumb will hurt. What could be more clear?

GREG: You drink the coffee at midnight – don't expect to sleep.

MAIKO: You have sex with the someone you don't know all that well – don't expect anything.

NGOZI: You look the stranger in the eye and you smile, you will probably be rejected.

GREG: You look the stranger in the eye, you avert your gaze and then you smile – life can proceed uninterrupted. Mystery solved.

(Ramsey Lewis fades out.)

MAIKO: Peace.

NGOZI: Exactly, peace.

GREG: Peace.

MAIKO: Peace. Peace. That's strange. Every time I say the word 'peace' my vision blurs.

GREG: Peace. Oh yeah.

NGOZI: Peace. Hey.

MAIKO: Peace.

GREG: Peace.

NGOZI: Peace.

MAIKO: Pppeeeaaaccceee. Well, that was weird. My vision blurred and then the objects of my vision seemed to be reconstituting as something else.

GREG: What?

MAIKO: I don't know. I ran out of air.

NGOZI: Hyperventilate for a bit, then try.

MAIKO: Okay. *(she hyperventilates)* Peeeeeeeeeeeeeeeeeeeeeeeeeeeeeeeeeaaaaaaaaaaaaaaaaaaaaaaaaaaaaaaaaaaaaaaaaaaaaaaaaaaaaaaaaaaaaaaaaaccccccccccccccccccccccccccccccccccccccccccccccccccccccccccccccccccccccceeeeeeeeeeeeeeeeeeeeeeeeeeeeeeeeeeeee.

NGOZI: That was a long time.

GREG: Yeah, you did good.

MAIKO: It was a long time.

NGOZI: What happened?

MAIKO: Well, my vision blurred –

GREG: Yeah?

MAIKO: And then everything seemed to reconstitute and I saw some people.

NGOZI: Really?!

MAIKO: Believe it or not.

GREG: I'd rather not.

NGOZI: Were you frightened?

MAIKO: I didn't feel frightened.

NGOZI: I think I would like to try it.

MAIKO: I propose we do it together.

GREG: I can't guarantee that I won't bail if I see a bunch of people.

NGOZI: Do it gently, don't make any sudden moves – who knows how that would be interpreted.

GREG: I'll try. On three.

MAIKO: On three.

NGOZI: One, two, three.

(They hyperventilate.)

MAIKO: Okay?

NGOZI: Okay. Breathe in deep. And go.

ALL: Peeeeeeeeeeeeeeeeeeeeeeeeeeeeeeeeeeeeeeeeeeeeeeeeeeeee eeeaaaaaaaaaaaaaaaaaaaaaaaaaaaaaaaaaaaaaaaaaaaa ccccccccccccccccccccccccccccccccccccccccccccccccccccccccc eeeeeeeeeeeeeeeeeeeeeeeeeeeeeeeeeeeeeeeeeeeeeeeeeeeeeeee.

MAIKO: Well? Did you see them?

GREG: Did you?

NGOZI: I saw something.

GREG: Did it look like people?

NGOZI: It did, sort of.

MAIKO: Were there any you felt attracted to?

NGOZI: I'm not really attracted to people anymore.

GREG: And yourself?

MAIKO: I feel the same way. And you.

GREG: People kind of disgust me.

MAIKO: Disgust?

GREG: Maybe that's too harsh. I think I feel a sort of pity bordering on disgust. But that's, of course, exactly how I feel about myself, so maybe it was just me I was encountering there at the far end of peace.

NGOZI: Maybe. They did look a lot like you.

GREG: Two ears?

MAIKO: Yeah.

GREG: Two eyes?

NGOZI: Yeah.

GREG: Two nostrils?

MAIKO: Yeah.

GREG: A small brain?

NGOZI: Smallest in the animal kingdom, proportionately speaking.

MAIKO: That does sound like you.

GREG: Sounds like you, too.

NGOZI: Well, maybe it was us after all.

GREG: I don't think I would be comfortable if it was anyone else.

MAIKO: Or anything else.

NGOZI: I don't think any inanimate object would be staring at us from the far end of peace.

MAIKO: You'd be surprised; there's this big jar following me everywhere.

GREG: Like a glass jar?

MAIKO: Yeah, like a regular, you know, pickle jar.

NGOZI: And it's following you?

MAIKO: I'll see it out of the corner of my eye. I'll be walking down the street and I'll stop to look at something.

GREG: A soap dish?

MAIKO: Could be. And the jar will stop. Sometimes back up, rolling slightly behind a newspaper box or something.

NGOZI: Is anything in the jar?

MAIKO: It's empty.

GREG: Have you tried to confront it?

MAIKO: I considered it, but what am I supposed to say to an empty jar?

NGOZI: True.

MAIKO: You know, what: 'Stop following me, your emptiness is getting me down' or –

GREG: Yeah, yeah.

NGOZI: You could tell it that following you around is not going to be very fulfilling so it should just cut its losses.

MAIKO: But how would I know? Maybe for an empty jar that kind of thing is fulfilling.

GREG: True.

NGOZI: I guess I'm not an empty jar.

MAIKO: That's too bad.

GREG: That is too bad.

NGOZI: Most of the time I'm a jar filled to the brim with sad and lonely confusion.

MAIKO: I'm a jar filled with an edgy kind of ugliness.

GREG: I'm a jar filled with a hatred toward the things that I can't change.

NGOZI: I'm filled with a hatred toward the very ground upon which I walk.

MAIKO: I can't keep my head screwed on straight.

GREG: I'm desperate for approval.

NGOZI: Love has never lasted and it's never been enough.

MAIKO: There's blood flowing from somewhere and I think it might be me.

GREG: I would crawl into a hole if I could find one that fit my head.

(Pause.)

MAIKO: Was it supposed to be like this or is this just the way it's become?

NGOZI: Hey, that question cost me a couple billion dollars on this dumb-ass game show the other night!

GREG: How did you answer it?

NGOZI: Well, I said that it just became this way.

MAIKO: And that was wrong?

NGOZI: Apparently.

GREG: I guess it's all in the way you look at it.

NGOZI: I could really have used that cash. I think the moment of stating the wrong answer may haunt me for a long time.

GREG: Probably the rest of your life.

MAIKO: I would think.

NGOZI: Great, haunted for the rest of my life.

GREG: I lived in a haunted house once – it wasn't so bad.

NGOZI: No?

GREG: The crazy ghost used to put too much salt in all the food. That was about it.

MAIKO: That doesn't sound so bad.

GREG: It really wasn't. Though at the time it could be very disruptive. There was one holiday feast that was totally ruined. All the food was just fresh out of the oven, all sitting on the table; the bird or whatever was golden brown beautiful –

NGOZI: Mm. That smells good.

GREG: There were all sorts of vegetables, lot of colours.

MAIKO: Green?

GREG: Lots of green.

MAIKO: Orange?

GREG: Yeah, orange. And brown: mashed roots, and butter, and sauces, and spices. Bread both light and airy and heavy and thick.

NGOZI: Meat?

GREG: Meats of all sorts.

MAIKO: Fish?

GREG: The table was swimming in them. We all sat down, adults at the kids' table, kids at the adults' table.

NGOZI: Uh-huh.

GREG: And someone took a bite and it was like –

MAIKO: Salty?

GREG: Inedible.

NGOZI: From this ghost?

GREG: There was a big fight; people were hungry, they had spent hours on this, tempers had been frayed, families had come from miles through bad weather and shitty immigration officials, new shoes had been purchased, blisters had formed, money had been spent – the whole nine yards.

MAIKO: And this was the moment all that suffering and conflict and confusion was to be traded for? This was the moment when love was supposed to flow?

GREG: Exactly.

NGOZI: So, what happened?

GREG: Well, some people around the table simply lost or misplaced their ability to laugh.

NGOZI: How does the story end?

GREG: Well, with an incident like that there is no ending, you know. I think some of the families around that table still haven't fully recovered.

MAIKO: All because of a salty ghost?

GREG: All because of a salty ghost.

NGOZI: Being haunted sounds terrible.

GREG: Oh, no, it can have benefits. The popcorn always tasted great. And shooting tequila was fun. You would just stick out your tongue and the ghost would lay down a patch of salt and away you'd go.

NGOZI: Do you guys have regular medical checkups?

MAIKO: Not regular – I just go when something's wrong.

GREG: Well, I gotta do the Pap smear thing every year.

MAIKO: I once had a friend and when she was menstrual my dreams would be especially vivid, often narrative, and full of false endings.

(Pause.)

NGOZI: Is that enough?

GREG: That's enough.

MAIKO: Yeah, that's enough.

(The lights gently fade as if it is the end but not completely. The actors can still be seen as they stand in dim light. Nat Raider's cover of Joni Mitchell's 'Woodstock' plays.)

MAIKO: Okay, you can open your eyes now.

NGOZI: That's it for the hug.

MAIKO: See, it wasn't so bad, was it?

GREG: I'll get the door.

(Greg steps off the stage and opens the doors to the theatre.)

NGOZI: Could we have some house? Thanks.

MAIKO: Who are we listening to, Nick?

NICK: It's Nat Raider covering Joni's 'Woodstock.'

MAIKO: Oh, that's right.

NGOZI: I like the line 'We are billion-year-old carbon.'

MAIKO: That is a good line.

GREG: So, that's about all you'll get from us today.

MAIKO: I hope you liked it.

GREG: You're free to go; there's a bar upstairs if you want a drink.

NGOZI: We'll probably be up there in a bit.

GREG: I hope it's not too cold outside.

MAIKO: The cold purifies.

GREG: That's true.

NGOZI: If anybody is interested, we want to extend an invitation to you to climb a little on the set before you take off.

GREG: Are we going to do that?

NGOZI: Darren thought it would be nice.

MAIKO: But you have to remove your shoes. You can leave them there.

NGOZI: Please come up if you like.

MAIKO: We also have to mention that, if you do, you do it at your own risk.

MAIKO: Of course. Our insurance won't cover you if you get hurt, so we can't let you climb too high, but it's nice just up here. JP, could you throw on some nice lights? *(He does so.)* Thanks.

NGOZI: Anybody interested?

MAIKO: It's a nice view from here. Come on up. If you like.

NGOZI: If not, then, like we said, you're free to go.

MAIKO: Or you can always just hang out for a drink; after all, it is good for your heart.

NGOZI: But do come up, it's nice.

GREG: Anybody interested?

(They stop speaking and wait to see what happens. If people come forward, the actors try to engage with them one-on-one, seguing out of performance mode, keeping the talk focused on the practical matter of getting the audience quickly onto the set. When the last audience member is leaving the set, the actors peel quietly away without saying anything. If, after a good period of time, the audience has no interest in climbing on the set, the actors look at each other, shrug, then walk away with a wave and a 'bye.')

The End

The Actors on *pppeeeaaaccceee*

Greg MacArthur

Nine thoughts on *pppeeeaaaccceee*:

1. If you've got an itch, scratch it.
2. People are odd, funny things. Enjoy them.
3. An honest, generous, attentive conversation is a rare thing. Enjoy this one.
4. Irony, sarcasm and ego have no place in this world.
5. A little glitter goes a long way.
6. Too much glitter gets all over your clothes and in your eyes and can be dangerous to ingest.
7. Cold feet are easier to warm than a cold heart.
8. This play is like a well-cooked piece of tofu: the more you taste it, the more normal it all seems.
9. This experience could change the way you look at the world and the people in it. Let it.

Maiko Bae Yamamoto

So I guess some important things to know about performing *pppeeeaaaccceee* are:

- If you think you're doing too much, you probably are.
- If you think you're not doing enough, well, that's a good place to start.
- Stay calm – or at least try to – and don't worry, it may feel absolutely terrifying for a moment, but you do – you really do – know the lines.
- Give over a bit and relax into it.
- Think of a warm summer afternoon by the lake, sitting on the dock at your good friend's cottage.

That's just what I did, and it seemed to work out all right.

pppeeeaaaccceee: it is what it is and there's nothing more to it than that. Keep it simple; you don't have to think ironically or in double meanings – the play does all that work for you. Just sit back, relax and enjoy the ride. This world is full of fabulous realities. It may make you a bit nervous or uncomfortable. But it's okay. Let yourself question honestly, be vulnerable – that's when the magic happens.

Like a two-year-old who questions everything and notices everything, like 'the sky is up, the music is in my ears, the moon is the plate, I love porridge.' They accept the answers as gospel truth. Love. Question. Love. Feel. Love. Listen. Love. Accept. Love. Let go. Love. pppeeeaaaccceee.

The Designers and Technical Staff on *pppeeeaaaccceee*

Lighting Designer Rebecca Picherack

When Darren and I began to talk about the lighting for *pppeeeaaaccceee*, his strongest impulses were for saturated colour and long cross fades. We wanted to generate the sensation of easiness, a soothing. The timescape of the play set some pretty clear parameters – from twilight to sunrise. In our first two workshops I described this conventionally, but a pure lighting workshop several months before the Six Stages production helped to open up my thinking.

We allowed ourselves to play unabashedly with light and shadow, colour, texture, movement, rhythm. There were many surprising discoveries – one of our favourites was creating the sense that an unseen image is retained in the retina. 'Hey, did you see that?' A gem for our next *pppeeeaaaccceee*.

During the lighting workshop we discussed how to allow the lights not only to be beautiful but also to contribute to the way the ideas of the play are being expressed, even to be a part of what the ideas are. The twilight/northern-lights dreamscape became the base for the conversation – but as Greg, Ngozi or Maiko would slip away into tangents, the lighting, often abruptly, would follow them. Sometimes the actors were fractured and contained in little light boxes, leaving a talking head in silhouette while the lights scrolled over chests and pelvises and faces. Are they one person? Are they contained in each other? We also used surprising sweeps of colour and shadows to help arc into new moods or ideas. Our main challenge with the lighting (and its coordination with Nick's sound and music) was to try to find a way to open people up, to approximate a waking dream state that may allow for a kinesthetic sensation that reaches back and forth between the stage and the audience. Like a warm group hug.

Sound Designer murr (Nick Murray)

When choosing the music for *pppeeeaaac-cceee,* I tried to keep in mind the sensitive nature of the dialogue; I kept the music really simple because of this.

I tried to imagine I was on the set of *Sesame Street* during the 70s inside a large nuclear reactor. The warm textures of Moog and Arp synthesizers helped to create this setting. Tension was created by using subtle rises in volumes as opposed to speed or rhythmic build. There is a sense of melancholy in the first half of the play and, as the action travels through the night to the dawn, the music gets a little happier. When working with the sound effects – crickets, birds, sirens – I maintained my use of vinyl, creating tight repetitive loops that had the warm crackle of old records.

Choreographer Sarah Chase

The simplicity of the staging of *pppeeeeeaaaccceee* appealed to me when I first read the script. I didn't want to interrupt the directness of it with a lot of fancy choreography. I was interested in working with a few simple series of gestures that would repeat at different times in the play – each time taking on a different context depending on what the actors were saying. I used the image of the point of reflection, a funnel of light coming to a point and then reversing itself, as a basic starting image for several of the gestures. This seemed to capture the essence of revolution, the moment at which energy comes together and transforms. I thought about how certain social movements have adopted symbolic hand gestures (the peace sign in the 1960s or the sieg heil movement from the Third Reich in Germany) and I tried to create a few hand signs that I thought could belong to the post-revolutionary world of *pppeeeaaaccceee*. The words of the song – 'When Love Goes Wrong' – that the three actors sing in the middle of the play was the source for the more complicated gesture series that recurs through the piece. Overall I was hoping to give the impression that the movement was happening to the actors, that it was some kind of radio signal they were picking up that came in and out of sync with the action.

Stage Manager John Patrick Robichaud

Directors tend to change their minds when working with a new script – they cut, uncut, shuffle, unshuffle, then finally cut and uncut again. Trying to keep track of those changes on paper, with Post-It notes and hastily scrawled arrows and parentheses, leads to a cluttered and confusing prompt script – the most important thing for a stage manager to keep clean and organized.

I try to use what technology I have available to me to keep things running smoothly and to cut down on the paper waste normally generated in the running of a rehearsal and production. When it comes to working on a new script, whether the playwright is in the room or not, the ability to immediately enter changes into a master copy is invaluable. Most of the work I've done in theatre has been on original pieces; my methods wouldn't necessarily work with a previously published script, but an SM will likely be able to find some kind of e-version of their script online. There are many websites that offer full folio versions of all of Shakespeare's commonly produced plays, for example. Other scripts might be found through some searching. If not, then you're out of luck – but it's worth the time to look.

I've found that I'm able to use Microsoft Word and Excel for OS X, along with Chronos's Sticky Brain and Organizer and Apple's TextEdit and Mail program, to completely replace a hard copy Stage Management book. My Titanium Powerbook's screen is large enough that I can have the script on one side of the screen and a page for blocking and cues on the other. I can make notes during a run using the Comment or Bookmark function in Word, keep an updated version of all cues in Excel, and e-mail rehearsal and show reports automatically at the end of the day – all without any paper at all. I can even use my TiBook as my running script in the booth, thanks to a piece of freeware I found called Nightvision X, designed by Stephen E. Hutson for use by amateur and professional astronomers. It controls the colour balance of the screen, turning it entirely red and making it ideal for low-light conditions. It's still possible to read everything on the screen, but the light level of the screen is such that it doesn't ruin your night vision – something that's very important for a stage manager – or cast a lot of excess light in the booth. In fact, when I was running pppeeeaaaccceee, the monitor for the lighting board cast more light, even with the brightness dimmed, than my TiBook. Nightvision X is a great piece of freeware, and while I don't think a theatrical use is what was intended, it's turned out that way for me.

This reliance on technology is not an approach that everyone is comfortable with – and with good reason. There does exist what many stage managers call the 'Mack Truck Principle': the idea that if the stage manager got hit by a truck on the way to the show, anyone else should be able to pick up their book and call the show. It makes a lot of sense. You never know what's going to happen, and it's the stage manager's job to think about all contingencies, or at least be able to deal with any problems that may arise. As such, I would never recommend not having a hard copy of your prompt script around. Make it accessible – print one up and leave it at the theatre, just in case. Let the theatre staff know where it is, so there's no time lost in trying to find it in case of an emergency. My approach is not to have no paper at all – just to make the job easier and lessen waste.

I've run many shows using my TiBook as my only script, and there's never been a problem. Mac OS X is an incredibly stable system – it *never* crashes, in my experience, and its flexibility makes it ideal for my job. It takes no time to transfer an entire show to a zip disk or to burn it onto a CD for storage. I imagine I'll even start giving my SM book to the theatre as a CD as opposed to a huge binder. Saves space for them, saves printing for me. I don't think the approach is for everybody, but I've found it's what works best for me.

Technical Director Trevor Schwellnus

The technical direction for *pppeeeaaaccceee* was fairly straightforward. The set is a cyclorama – a single large piece of fabric sweeping down from the ceiling – a couple of risers, some foam and a ladder. It was fairly easy to set up the basics – the devil was in the finishing touches.

I felt that lighting was the principal concern, really, for a play about three people who do little but converse. The challenge lay in how to create a sense of progression when conflict is absent and characters don't really develop so much as become more familiar. Lighting filled the dramatic place that narrative usually occupies. The changes in its patterns – in the strong, constantly morphing colours of the cyclorama wash, in the crisp shifting squares of front light, and in the projected effects – distinguished sections of the play when action did not, supporting the movement of the discussion onstage with an energetic visual progression.

For me, then, these visual elements had to be very tight. The huge piece of fabric would overstretch where it was most exercised during the show and thus needed to be easily adjusted from one performance to the next. As for the special effects, Darren had been mulling over the idea of projecting shadows of spinning plastic toys on the fabric, but our experiments were unsatisfactory; we instead used an overhead projector to project the shadows of several dozen live crickets over most of its surface. The crickets were reluctant performers – they didn't swarm quite enough. A tiered plexiglass case might have worked better than the insect 'aquarium' we purchased (such is the difficulty of late changes to the design). The other complication was in getting Mark, the production manager of Theatre Passe Muraille, to allow live crickets into his theatre. 'The first time one gets out,' he said, swinging his arms in a terminal arc, 'it's over.'

Crickets aside, however, my experience with Mammalian Diving Reflex was of a mature and dynamic group of artists who approach their work with a sense of humour and curiosity. This is the kind of play that pushes theatre into exploring performance styles that resonate in fresh ways with the audience – and which the big companies will never understand.

Nina Okens, costume designer, dresses the set

pppprinciples for a pppost-revolutionary ppproducing ppparadigm

(or, how to change the world without resorting to pppropppopppaganda)

by Producer Naomi Campbell

Producing *pppeeeaaaccceee* was really no different than producing any other play: a juggling act, a mathematical puzzle, a pile of paperwork, a wish or two (fingers crossed), favours gathered and given, and then the run; oh so brief, so ephemeral, and over before you could say 'pppeeeaaaccceee.'

I could discuss the tasks required to produce this or any other play: the grant writing, deal making, budgeting, casting, contracting, marketing, set building, costuming; the technical challenges (the cricket wrangling!); the discoveries and the disappointments. I could bemoan the fact that there's never enough time for me to just sit in rehearsals and soak it all in; that I am probably missing the moments when it really happens. Or am I? One could argue that the moments that make those moments possible are just as important to the process and the product as any camaraderie that occurs in the rehearsal hall – they just might not be as entertaining.

One of the advantages of working independently, without the responsibilities of a venue or a staff, is that we don't have to look at our work first and foremost as a commercial venture. As long as it is self-sustaining, as long as we are frugal and don't spend any money that we don't have, we're OK. Our fragile civilization needs artists who won't capitulate to market forces; I'm not interested in participating in that big commercial market where you lure the audience into the theatre by inundating them with flashy ads that cost more than our entire show budget. Rather than seeing our inability to compete in that realm as a failing, we try and rely on a standard of work that will compel an audience to exist.

The best marketing for poor theatre is excellence and originality. It is our own high standards that we must rely on to inspire the audience to work on our behalf. Ideally, the work literally speaks for itself, inducing a rush of word of mouth. And I rely on something I call karma marketing – if we work really hard and ask difficult questions, if we make it look and sound and taste fantastic and unusual, if we provoke the audience so that they feel like they need to talk to their friends about it afterwards, if we treat people right all through the process, then the audience will just show up.

With *pppeeeaaaccceee* we at Mammalian Diving Reflex worked very hard at the 'treating people right' part of the equation. We aspired to create a little post-revolutionary enclave in our practice and in our process. We were constrained, of course, by the conventions and assumptions of early twenty-first century Canadian theatre, but we tried to do it all just a little bit differently nevertheless. We paid everyone as much as we possibly could; we made the work week civilized; we covered the treats and the coffee; we tried to create an environment where everyone felt empowered to speak about all aspects of the work while still maintaining their expertise in their own areas; we tried to listen; and we held a great opening night party that was warm and generous and pleasing to both the company and the crowd. Generosity around people's lives and their needs is critical. It is clear that we can't change the world with a play, so the challenge is to create both work and a way of working that alters the perspective of everyone that it touches even just a little bit; and to create a work environment that is as close to the way it should be in an ideal world as we can possibly afford.

Producing in poverty, every penny is heavier, and its weight is philosophical as well as fiscal; how it is spent, on what and to whom, becomes all the more important. Creating a team of people who you trust and respect, who have ownership of their contributions, means that when the financial resources are meagre they will pitch in. Then, when the resources are more plentiful, it's important to pay those same people well, so that their sweat investment ultimately pays off. It is a shame, but it's true, that a lot comes down to money; that the desire to make the work better all around can be codified in cash, although loyalty, respect and understanding do go a long way, as does grace, and good will.

Yvonne Ng and her artwork for pppeeeaaaccceee

We save money by ensuring that the favour bank is full at the beginning of rehearsals – that we've helped people out when they've asked, that we've been generous with our time and our expertise so that it will come back to us when we need it most. Assets are there to be shared in a theatre of barter where integrity is the most important commodity. Our resources are multiplied by our good will, and while we can't buy the big ads, we can try to ensure that everyone we know wants to speak enthusiastically about us and our work. Toronto's independent theatre community could not produce radical work without everyone helping each other out. We don't function as a group of competitors, but rather as comrades, bent on the same mission. And every audience member that Mammalian Diving Reflex brings back to the theatre becomes a potential audience member for others producing radical work.

There is an expectation of criticism in the theatre – not just from our formal critics but also from each other, both directly and more casually behind each other's backs. We rationalize this behaviour as a form of analysis and self-preservation, but it is our biggest failure. We must attempt to function outside competition, both professionally and in our daily interactions. We work together to make theatre – this is our greatest contribution to the human dynamic. We tell old stories in new ways by working in co-operation with others, and to taint that with petty grievances reduces our efforts.

The dramaturgical challenge that *pppeeeaaaccceee* poses is one the world would benefit from addressing: can we get the daily drama fix we need without conflict? Do we diminish ourselves by giving in to the lazy dramaturgy of 'the good guys vs. the bad guys'? Can we thrive without the story of good and evil – why aren't we ready to leave that one behind? By inserting a third voice into the conversation the simple dichotomy is broken, and a discussion is created where someone has to compromise. Ideally, in the real world, all of us would compromise more often, and we would all gain from the experience. In the theatre, as in life, we would all be better off with something a little more sophisticated than 'me vs. you' as the foundation of our lives and our work.

And we do want to affect real life. Our catch phrase 'Ideal entertainment for the end of the world' expresses our desire to facilitate the end of *this* world – the world of outrageous disparity and despair, of greed and anger and plain old bad moods. By extension, our work is intended to support and contribute to the beginning of the new – and finally equitable – world. And while the work of MDR and the work that I love the best could be described as political theatre, we have tried to come up with other ways of articulating that idea, so we don't scare a potential audience with the notion of something prescriptive, something good for you but not very tasty. Political or popular theatre has a reputation for being rough and ready, simple and theatrically unsophisticated, which is the last thing we are interested in. Something more devious, more subversive, is required and a sense of humour about our own didacticism is more effective than info-laden polemic. By keeping the theatrical standards high we can sweep the audience into another state of mind, dazzle them with beauty and shock them with magic; induce an altered state so that the observer becomes a participant in the work and is implicated in our process. The art of theatre and the constituency that's interested in political and philosophical content need not contradict each other; we do everyone a disservice with that assumption.

However, if we reveal too much about what we are trying to accomplish and what the work is about, it won't have the same effect on the audience. We can't give it all away beforehand. There is an inherent problem in talking about a show that is 'unlike anything else you've ever seen.' If you're trying to sell something that's almost impossible to describe, that you don't even want to describe because if you do you'll ruin the experience, then you're left with a crazy marketing challenge. I would describe *pppeeeaaaccceee* by saying that it's about life after the revolution and pretty much leave it at that. There is a beautifully optimistic notion at work in that statement. The implication that there will be a revolution in the foreseeable future was one of the real pleasures of telling people about the show. The reply 'Which revolution?' allowed me the delighted comeback 'You know ... the revolution,' as if it were as inevitable as the sunset and the sunrise that follows. The gift of *pppeeeaaaccceee* was its inherent optimism – that there is a world after the revolution, and that it will be good.

Mammalian Diving Reflex's particular process is no doubt greatly influenced by a domestic idiosyncrasy. Darren I and live so close to each other that we meet a lot in our pyjamas; we share meals and lend onions, apples and cups of rice; we pick up things at the store for each other and borrow quarters for the laundry. The shared wall between our apartments lends a special intimacy to our process; it means that we are both very aware of what it takes out of the other to do our jobs, and how much our personal lives cannot be extricated from our work.

In moments of insecurity I wonder if it is fear of success that feeds our desire to be peripheral, that we might be radical as a way to avoid the complications arising from a bigger audience. Is our contempt for the mainstream just armour to protect us from our own obscurity? Do we dare toy with the tantalization of success, break the poverty paradigm and try to reap the rewards of a bigger pool of people who follow our work? Or would success leave us bereft of our story? I hope not, and for now my doubts pass and I sustain the delusion that theatre can help to change the world even if it keeps us out of the mainstream.

So, how do we make theatre and a difference out of the same material? A few days ago I was at a candlelight vigil in anticipation of World War III, and as I was looking around the circle I was struck by the role that artists, and specifically the theatre, can play. An invitation was made by the informal leader for songs or poems from the group. People seemed to want to speak, to sing, to pray, but shyness held many back. It was a theatre worker and a musician who stepped forward and led the group. And as the audience joined in, they fell away from their audienceness and we were united. If we can achieve that inside the theatre and in the world at large, then we have truly succeeded in our task.

Theatre itself can't change people, but it can inspire change in people, and it can drive them to act. At best it is catalytic; if we can consistently challenge people to transform their world view then we are truly on to something. The more we understand about the things we don't understand, the better. And radical work makes room for more radical work. It makes room for more people, more ideas, more interconnectedness, more support, more art and more hope.

Even a Broken Clock Occasionally Tells the Correct Time: Theatre and Revolution

by Darren O'Donnell

This is addressed to those theatre artists who would like to participate in the demise of current economic structures, whatever you want to call them: capitalism, corporate capitalism, corporate antimarkets, global oligarchies ... whatever ... you know who I mean. This is addressed to those who, sheepishly or otherwise, wish to be revolutionaries. Everybody else, please stop reading.

The newspapers have been shrinking their coverage of theatre over the past couple of years. Can we blame them? If theatre's not relevant, it's not relevant; they're not about to start publishing a section on knitting, as popular as it might be – after all, both are fun for the participants and the recipients always seem grateful, but as far as wider social impact ... I've seen some really nice sweaters.

Since the 80s there's been an intense commodification of art; most artists have begun to think like business people. Problem is, theatre resists this. Filming theatre doesn't often work, an audio recording is useless, and playscripts will never reach a mass market. Because of this, most intelligent artists committed to strongly engaging with the world have no interest in theatre. Why speak into a microphone that's unplugged?

However, working in mediums that are, indeed, plugged in often means getting trapped in institutions that merely maintain the status quo: radical art on display in bourgeois cages. But theatre hangs out in the interstices where nobody's really watching – the perfect place for the embarrassed revolutionary to begin her practice. And what better time than now?

Nobody predicted the fall of communism, just like nobody will predict the fall of capitalism. One day things will just fly apart and we'll have to put them back together. It could happen in five years or in five hundred – nobody knows. The greed, stupidity and duplicity of the corporate world is leading me to believe it will be sooner rather than later, but, truly, who knows. Once a dismantling begins, there will a lot of confusion and chaos, but there will also be the space and the need for theatre to participate in forming whatever comes next. In order to get ourselves ready, the embarrassed revolutionary should be getting his own house in order. Here are a few revolutionary suggestions. They're not particularly new and they may very well be stupid, but please consider them the dumb ideas that may lead us to the good ones.

1 Forget about your tired life and tedious artistic aspirations and, instead, engage with your community on practical problems. Become a great citizen and then, if there's still time, a great artist.

2 Stop talking about films all the time.

3 Accept the fact that, since you're living in the economic centre, you likely understand NOTHING of the situation; your consciousness has been propagandized into oblivion.

4 Accept the fact that neoliberalism has brought about a degree of disparity, injustice and atrocity unparalleled in the history of the world. And it's intensifying as you read this.

5 In your own theatre practice, address the rampant white supremacy that still strangles almost all theatre in Europe and Neo-Europe: Canada, the US, Australia, New Zealand.

6 Theatre people are legendary for being horny, attention-starved showoffs. Keep the legend alive. Try to avoid traditional two-person monogamous units; they are particularly potent at reproducing problematic power dynamics. Atypical romantic arrangements will contribute to destabilizing the status quo. But you must do this honestly and openly. Enjoy yourself loudly and guiltlessly or, since we're a bunch of actors, at least pretend that you're guiltless. Eventually, like all choreography, you'll get the hang of it.

Troy O'Donnell, assistant director

7 Emphasize the particular over the universal. Anyone can talk about love, death and loss. Talk, instead, about this historical moment.

8 When capitalism eventually unravels, leadership will come from those who have been fighting much longer than us. We will need to learn a lot and quickly. Cultural collaborations with the so-called third worlds will be more helpful than those with the EU, the UK or the USA.

9 Know that techies, box-office staff, and front of house are collaborators as intrinsic and essential to the total experience as actors, designers and directors.

10 Make sure that the transition from the preshow state to the show itself is seamless. An aborted preshow song tells the audience that the real world has finished and the play is now beginning. But, for the embarrassed revolutionary, the world is the show and the show

is the world. Make sure the play is upon them before they've had a chance to cast away their lives.

11 Always ask, 'Who do the lights and sound represent and what do they have to say?'

12 Get rid of post-show clapping so the audience doesn't have a chance to jar the electrical effects of your work out of their bodies by repeatedly smashing their palms together. It's no accident that the more effective the play the more effort the audience puts into numbing their hands. Transferring the burden of feeling from their heart to their hands is simply a way of ducking responsibility.

Acknowledgements

I would like to acknowledge the dramaturgical contributions of all the actors who worked on the *pppeeeaaaccceee* over the years: Julian Diego, Saskia Dunn, Holly Lewis, Greg MacArthur, Ngozi Paul, Simmi Shukla, Nicole Stamp and Maiko Bae Yamamoto, as well as those of Naomi Campbell, Sarah Chase, Daniel MacIvor, Nick Murray, Troy O'Donnell, Rebecca Picherack and JP Robichaud. I would also like to acknowledge Layne Coleman and the Theatre Passe Muraille Playwrights Unit where *pppeeeaaaccceee* was first read.

I would also like to acknowledge the support of Buddies in Bad Times Theatre, the Toronto Arts Council, the Ontario Arts Council, the Canada Council for the Arts, the Laidlaw Foundation and the Six Stages Festival.

– Darren O'Donnell

About the Playwright

Darren O'Donnell is a writer, director, designer, actor and the artistic director of Mammalian Diving Reflex. His plays include *White Mice, Boxhead, Radio Rooster Says That's Bad, Over* and *Who Shot Jacques Lacan?*. He was the 2000 recipient of the Pauline MacGibbon Award for directors and he has been nominated for a number of Dora Awards for his writing, directing and acting and has won for design. *Inoculations*, a collections of his plays, was published in 2001 by Coach House Books, which will also be publishing his first novel, *Your Secrets Sleep With Me,* in spring 2004. Visit www.mammalian.ca for more information.

Typeset in Sabon
Printed and bound at the Coach House on bpNichol Lane, 2003

Edited and designed by Alana Wilcox
Cover art by Yvonne Ng
Photo of cover art by See Spot Run Inc.
Back cover photo by John Lauener (www.johnlauenerphotography.com)
Cover design by Rick/Simon
Typeface on the cover by beehive design
Performance photos on pages 28, 33, 49, 53, 55, 62, 73, 77, 96, 115 and 117 by John Lauener
Rehearsal photos on pages 13, 16, 58, 88 and 95 by Rick/Simon
Rehearsal photos on pages 44, 52, 78, 80, 91, 93, 98, 100, 123, 124, 125,128, 129, 131 and 137 by Darren O'Donnell
Rehearsal photos on pages 20, 38, 65, 99, 107 and 127 by Troy O'Donnell

For information on producing this play, please contact Darren O'Donnell at darren@mammalian.ca.

To join the Coach House e-mail list, write mail@chbooks.com

Coach House Books
401 Huron Street (rear) on bpNichol Lane
Toronto, Ontario
M5S 2G5

416 979 2217
1 800 367 6360

www.chbooks.com